Thomas Brackmann

Into the Unkn

Printed in Germany
BoD - Books on Demand, Norderstedt

ISBN 978-3-7460-1790-7

Into the Unknown

6 years globetrotting across all continents to boldly go where I have never gone before...

Buy a ticket! Jump on a plane! Travel all over the world! Meet interesting people! Experience at first hand, the culture, and diversity across each country! That's what has driven my inner spirit for the past six years.

During my travels I have experienced some eye opening things, some spectacular events, some things that have brought a tear to my eye, and some that have given me life lasting memories. One of my great delights has been telling people about my travels and experiences after I had returned. Usually I would set up a short presentation to friends, and interested colleagues, over a lunch, or evening buffet.

My travelling is done at an outrageous pace, visiting more than 30 countries each year, at times staying only for a few hours or days, before flying out to the next destination. That is my way. I was driven by the speed of it all. Each year I tried to include at least 20 new countries to my journeys across the globe to expand my knowledge and experience.

As Barney in the TV Show "How I met your mother" usually says, "New is always better!" I tried to apply this rule for all my travelling. The "New" was always interesting for me, primarily to tick off another new country from my list, but mainly to experience its environment and culture.

When the urge first came upon me to start travelling in 2010, I just wanted to see Australia, or South America, once in my life. I was so impressed by it all that I developed a personal goal to travel to all 193 countries recognized by the UN. I thought that if I achieve that, I might go further, and travel to other breakaway countries, and territories. The sky is not the limit! Above 100 Kilometers space is calling! Who knows what the future will bring? "Richard Branson! Are you listening?"

In order to reach my goal I tried to avoid using my leave for going home to Germany, or to the same countries twice. For me that would have been a waste of my scarce amount of money and time. Ok! "Wasting" sounds quite harsh, but with my goal to visit all these countries, I needed to focus, and calculate with my limited cash and vacation days what was possible. I did not want to have a gap year, a sabbatical, or take a long period of unpaid leave from my job. I wanted to travel while working and receiving an inward cash flow to jump from journey to journey every 4 to 5 weeks.

There were exceptions of course: Family visits (Mama is calling), weddings, and, sadly funerals at which I had to be present. These trips in themselves provided me with additional opportunities to tell stories about my travels. Apart from just visiting the countries, I wanted to leave a "Thomas Brackmann" footprint in the places I visited, by doing something extra ordinary. So: I have taught Judo in the wilderness of Kirgizstan, completed an Ironman triathlon in New Zealand, and did one-arm pushups in Machu Picchu. I invested some of my hard earned cash in a British pub in Romania, and I am planning to support a school project in Honduras. There is always something going on with me. Patience isn't one of my strengths; sitting still is something I only do in an airplane, when heading off to the next country on my list.

This explains the reason why you will find that some of the stories in this book are rapidly told, somewhat interrupted and at times not in the best native tongue, Oxford English or grammar. It is a reflection of the pace of my life! Perhaps I should take a tip from colleagues, and slow down a little!

I just focus on getting the best prices for my trips, dreaming of my next travel destinations, training for another Ironman, or Marathon! And Hey! Travelers style "Broken English" is the language of our time, right! Or?

Special thanks for Colin, Sana and Ali supporting me in this book adventure.

List of content

2010 – Kick off!

Saudi Arabia – Let's go!

Lucky me! Due to fortunate circumstances I got hired via a head hunter for a superb job in Riyadh, capital city of the Kingdom of Saudi Arabia in July 2010. A 2-years contract without social insurance. Awesome! No more suffering from freelance earnings and the German weather conditions. Yippee! No Tax! Paid accommodation, provided car, swimming pool, a gym, 30 days vacation and 11 public holidays. Sounded great! I thought I was dreaming, but then every high has its lows, which I soon discovered. Tough for a European! No alcohol, no bars, no cinemas, no theatres, strict gender segregation of single people, the death penalty! And, and, and. A challenging environment! I thought as an Afghanistan experienced veteran that it shouldn't be a problem for me. Or should it?

Beirut or Singapore – I just needed to get away

After surviving the 3 month probation period in my new job, finally, time for my first vacation experience. Decisions, decisions! Was it going to be Beirut, or Singapore, both were places I always wanted to go. Both exotic, mystical, big city flair! My best study buddy Stefan said to me: "Forget Singapore, the parties are better in Beirut!"

Armed with a long to-do list provided by my friends and colleagues, I started my first Middle East adventure. Ok! Great! Tallyho! But it was not to be! Off to a bad start with six hours delay at the airport in Riyadh. A long wait in the departure lounge together with hundreds of people from all over the world: India, Pakistan, Ethiopia, UK, etc., etc. Air-conditioners were off! Either broken or malfunctioning, resulting in rising temperatures, and the resonating aroma, and smells, from each corner of this planet, with every culture having its own special flavor. And me, stuck in the middle of this cloud. Great!

No money – No honey!

Finally! Arrival! Touchdown in a sleepy drowsy mode. The first shock! Neither my ATM, nor Credit cards were working. 3 bank cards, 3 different ATM machines, no luck! No injection of local cash into my pocket. Here I was in a foreign city, feeling frustrated, when an old phrase came into my mind; No money! No honey! As in every Third World Airport there are uncountable taxi drivers who want to make business, who want to rip off the naive travel rookie, and so they did with me. 50 US-Dollar to the city center. I remember thinking: Never mind! Its holiday time. I was not exactly a poor backpacker, having to count every penny. Plus, my probation time was over. Two years Saudi salary ahead! Yippi! Let's go into the Paris of the Middle East.

War zone! Or party place?

OMG! What am I doing here? Holes in the walls, buildings in ruins, people begging on the streets. Did I make a mistake? What was running through my head was a mix of pictures from my missions in Afghanistan, Kosovo, and Bosnia. I became a little angry with my friend who recommended Beirut as a great party place. And still: No injection of new money in my pocket. Therefore: March, march to a world bank. Someone must be able to help me there, I believed. First the (fresh) money then the (party) honey!

Travel boy meets Bank girl

HSBC – the great hope for party funding. It would have been a shame to be without cash in one of the greatest party places on this planet. With eyebrows bouncing and "smiler-alert" sitting behind the desk, I saw the first female without a veil for the last three months. I thought to myself no wonder a man can be getting weak and melty. Aside of providing me 500 US Dollars fresh cash, her telephone number also came along. A date in two days! City guide included. Check! To quote and old English phrase: "Easy Peasy! Japanese." Maybe there is some add-on possible. But then, it was off to the hotel for a shower, beer, and then bed time. The day was exhausting enough, physically and mentally!

God is a DJ

No sleep tonight Thomas: I met a fellow travel guy from Canada in the lobby of Hotel Napoleon. Quickly, I placed an order for 2 beers, but that was not yet the final story. He had already arranged with a mix of locals and other travelers for evening dinner, and partying. Barhopping was the new mission of the night! Some different clubs and drinks later, we were finally rocking at the techno temple "BO18". One Swedish colleague had recommended it before my trip, it was a good tip. Another check in the box on my to-do list. Best techno music in da house. Felt like in old Berlin Techno Love Parade times. Spontaneously, I created the headline of this section in remembrance of the nineties music group Faithless who sang "God is a JD". I met him that night in Beirut! Really! Beirut is not only the party center of the Middle East, but is the location to go from other parts of the world. In other metro poles of the world party is on only happening at weekends, but in Beirut, the fiestas are on every single day.

Dancing until around 4 the morning, still up to speed, thanks to a Red Bull and Vodka mix which kept me flying with some extra kicks. Then finally in the morning back to the hotel, crashing into 2 hotly dressed ladies in the elevator. I figured 2 call girls, my only thought was: There are elevator pitches and elevator bitches! And when they knock at the room door later on coz the original customer refused them, sleeping is not possible anymore.

Damascus for a Day

After a short night departure at 7 in the morning. Ready, steady, go to Damascus, capital of Syria. In 2017 it is a warzone and not so safe. Back then, it was rather friendly and ok. I had booked the trip after my arrival in Beirut. Agenda: bus tour, border crossing, Central Square, mosque, souk, lunch, and return to Beirut, It was a tough schedule. Lack of sleep was to be compensated for on the bus ride. I had a shock awaking: Damascus looked not welcoming, poor, many damaged buildings, and tourist hotspots were different and not appealing. The best overall was the big mosque. This holy building was wide, bright and shiny with very nice decoration. Good for selfie pictures and panoramic shots. But what else could I do? Either I was still too sleepy, or the city was really not that overwhelming. I didn't see any other highlight worth visiting. To be fair, 1 day was not that much, but my first impression wasn't that great.

Sleepless in Lebanon

The following days: Party hopping from "BO18" to drinking bars on Hamra or Gemmayze Street. Apart from the nights out, different rendezvous with the bank girl, and a good night's sleep, I managed some sightseeing bus and car tours with some friendly Lebanese people I met. When I managed to stay awake, I could spot ancient historical Greek or Roman buildings outside Beirut, Awesome! I was also informed that Lebanon also offers some great beach clubs, and ski resorts. Definitely, sometime in the future, I need to come back for a wedding or layover to discover the beaches and the skiing opportunities as a side travel dish. Bon appetite! But for the beginning of my travel journeys I need to explore the rest of the world.

Sleep is overrated

This rough week in Beirut has shown: Sleep is overrated, especially in the night. In party mega centers such as Beirut, you can stay awake for 24 hours and beyond. Of course, the body needs rest, but with a clever rest-energy-management program, anything is possible. The body needs sleep from time to time, but 2 days techno dancing through the night in clubs is as the same as an army exercise for 48 hours. Same, same, but different as the people in Thailand say. Lesson learned: it's a must, to have 1000 USD in cash already before arriving to prevent any surprises when landing and finding no ATM or Credit cards are working – mostly outside Europe.

2011 – Party around the world

Up in the air in Hong Kong

One week in Singapore and Hong Kong in spring 2011. Before going to work in the Middle East I knew both only from TV. After choosing Beirut over Singapore in 2010 it was time for the double pack of the Far East. The former British colony of Hong Kong would also easily offer the Chinese country point, and tick the box in my travel book without any visa issues. Great! Together with my travel buddy Julian we went on with the travel planning. Quickly we discovered it is cheaper to fly the triangle flight against the clock: Riyadh-Singapore-Hong Kong-Riyadh. That saved us around 400 Dollars. I wanted to memorize this fact for future travels. It takes only some minutes to check this out online when booking.

We were nearly blown away by the sight of the high skyscrapers in combination with the narrow streets of Hong Kong, I felt very small and lost. At night the lights of the city looked amazing, with all the thousands of small windows in the high buildings shining like sparkling stars. All these windows stand for small apartments as the property prices are astronomic. Consequently we also had a little room in our hotel, only 10 square meters, but it was equipped with all the necessary items for a 4 Stars standard. The first two days we were intoxicated, full of alcohol, resulting from intercultural bar hopping and nightclubs. Singapore Sling was calling as well. The climate during these days was fog and rain but it did not stop me discovering cultural sites, including the big Buddha statue which helped me to come down from my high and detox – at least mentally.

Macao – The winner takes it all

Hong Kong to Macau in a heartbeat. The distance was pretty short. It was not on our agenda but when we recognized that Macau is the Las Vegas of the Far East – we needed to give it a try. The golden Casino was our place to be and to gamble. As the only customers, we were more than welcome, and we both gambling rookies trying our luck. Even trying to figure out certain logic behind roulette wheel, to spot a trend in the numbers, and to take a win home. After nearly 15 minutes of studying, I still hadn't made my move, while Mister Julian was already the lucky one, having 200 US Dollar winnings in his pocket. Several hours and drinks later, he left the Casino with 500 Dollars. I only got

100 but we figured gambling while travelling could increase the travel budget, or not. Lessons learnt!

Travel business as unusual

The first two trips abroad to Beirut and Hong Kong demonstrated to me the great opportunities of travelling. As they say in Star Trek, "to boldly go where no one has gone before, and discover strange new worlds". That was the spirit I wanted to follow, and I figured, 3 days in a place would be enough to get amazed and surprised by these new places. In addition, when planning the trips and preparing the agenda of things to see, eat and drink, I also needed to plan the required energy resources, such as when to sleep, when to boost myself with coffee, alcohol, or carbohydrates, to be awake in critical or important moments, and using the down time (plane, bus etc.) for sleeping and relaxing. Average I calculated: 3 days per country makes 2 cities. I planned sleeping for a minimum amount of time, especially during the night. I estimated that costs for transport, food, and drinks could be reduced as well, or better planned. For getting spoilt in evening, a six-pack from the liqueur store and drinking on empty stomach saves money and gives a faster road to a drunken status. In addition, overall fitness for rapid travelling is a must. I haven't seen fast travelers being fat. For my own safety, I could build up on a black belt judo skill level for self-defense, and some running skills to make a quick exit. So: Well prepared to conquer the world. Still so much to see, to visit, to explore! Yallah!

Via Kuwait to incredible India

The beginning of July: My birthday. After 1 year in the sandpit of Saudi Arabia I aimed for special treat. Somehow I ended up with India. Therefore I booked as a layover the little country of Kuwait, northeast of Saudi Arabia. Kuwait – a classical 1 day country. Nothing much to see! Attractiveness: Zero! Before flying I asked a colleague if he had ever been to Kuwait before, and if he could recommend some spots to visit. The English man just said: "Yes dude, 1990 together with my military unit we fought for freedom down there". I didn't expect this answer. Nevertheless, he recommended the local national museum. Indeed that was the highlight of Kuwait City, the capital. The invasion by Iraqi forces was displayed in a professional and detailed style. It was impressive, with sound effects, smoke, and night lights. Bam! Bum! Bang! Other sightseeing spots: Kuwait Twin Towers, with a great view above the corniche while having a coffee. Another highlight close to the Hotel Radisson Blu: An old wooden sailing boat has been reconstructed and adjusted to host two spectacular restaurants. One was inside the belly of the boat. The other one was just underneath it, below the water line. In both they offered Arabic – Mediterranean food, and non–alcoholic beverages. Kuwait is also a dry country – no alcohol allowed like in Saudi. But upgraded due to the fact that women are allowed to drive.

Through the monsoon to the inner me

After this short intermezzo in Kuwait, it was time to continue the journey, off to India. As the advertisement states: "Incredible India", strangely, it was a cheap trip. Only after booking I realized July is the peak of the rain season. So I got worried about spending my birthday full of rain. But if you are getting Ayurveda treatment, monsoon rain season cannot harm you. That was the saying of a colleague. So I aimed for relaxing treatments, to find my inner self and spirit. Maybe walking on my karma pathway to find the higher state of consciousness – at the beach, or in a bar, wellness temple, or pool, while dancing under the blue moon, or in a drunken state. OOOOOOhmmmmm!

Indian diarrhea vs. big city beats

Three to four days I had planned. First Mumbai and then Goa to conclude the Indian sub-continent – ridiculous of course. But due to extrapolation and deriving from old to new – it should be possible. Big cities like Mumbai you can find worldwide: History meets modernity. Along the way there is culture with temples, Ghandi Museum, Gateway of India, churches, shrines etc., poor and rich people, ugly ones and yoyoba beauties, patient poles and vibrant quarters. As an Indian add on you will get either food poison or diarrhea. You haven't been to India if you didn't get one or both sicknesses. I made that tick in the box already on my inbound flight. Holla Karacho! Effect: Easy peasy mostly bread related food in following days of toilet thunder. But in compensation: Lots of Imodium. The good thing with all the shitting – weight loss and no real appetite!

Terror traffic in Mumbai

There were several terror attacks shortly before my arrival in Mumbai. But that calmed me down. Why? According to different books and stories about bombings in World War 1 the safest places on the battle field were the bomb craters. A bomb or grenade never detonates in the same place again. Therefore I focused on the previously attacked hotel and restaurants. All peaceful though. Great! But the traffic was killing. It is easier to get murdered between Lorries, speeding cars, rickshaw bikes and other motor vehicles on these streets. Indian traffic survivors will fall asleep once they drive in bella Roma in Italy.

The mercy of the German origin

I was a bit anxious when three young Indian fellows wanted to show me the way to the highlights of the city – for cash of course. I thought they will lead me to a backyard and kill me softly and slowly. At least robbing was an option. Nevertheless the force of Judo and other self-defense skills was with me and I could power up by showing confidence. Alert was on! Luckily we had a nice conversation about Indian lifestyle and art of surviving in Mumbai. I dived deeper into the culture of this Indian sub-continent. Poverty and the daily cash-in was priority number one for the three boys. They live from begging on the streets and offering tourist guide services. At the end I gave some valuables to them and was again happy of my German birth and the German passport. Other people haven't had so much luck being born in the right place. In moments like these you become humble and appreciate what you have got.

Indian Ibiza with Spa spirit

Next stop Goa. The cheap hotel in a quiet area outside the party center of Goa was not ready for me. Like in other hotels worldwide check in time is around lunch time. Me, the non-patient person wanted just to relax in a decent place. So I directly ordered the taxi to take me to the city center and get me into a better hotel, but, I quickly changed my mind, since I believed as it's my birthday, I should have some luxury. Next! Off to the party place in the north of Goa. In a better hotel I found a 100 Euro suite. Since it was the rain season I got a special 3 days package and discount. Same, same, but different for a hotel with connected Spa. Three hours of Ayurveda treatment for the next 3 days, for only 120 Euro, Touché! Made my day! 9 different treatments each time: Full body massage, hot honey pack, steam bath, head massage, feet relaxation, scrubbing and so on. Great birthday days to come.

Couple up to get in

Totally relaxed after day 1 three hours pamper pack, I felt ready to dance the night away. An evening in the disco in downtown, I believed so. Failure! Entry only with company! Couples only! While men and women meet on western dance floors in the night clubs, or bars, in India you need to acquire your plus one already in the morning, after breakfast. Especially for single travelers the motto is: If you want to eat, or dance in the night, you need to hunt in the morning. Simple is that! Mostly, the dance temples are closed, especially for single peeps. Even my white touristic face, exotic bonus didn't help. Ok! I didn't try it with hard dollars. Travel lesson learnt: Next time, getting prepared already in the morning! Travelling forms!

The last beer was bad – like always

So, I had to find a shabby place to get pissed, since I was a bit pissed off! Getting passing the evening with some drinks. On my way home I ended up drinking in a simple beach pub style bar. That was all I could remember. OMG! What have I done? On the next morning the bar owner welcomed me with the demand for a cleaning service payment for the previous night. Now I know I couldn't remember. He told me what happened the night before. I got too many drinks, too fast, and created a massacre with the rest room. I guess like always, the last beer wasn't the best quality. However with some bad feelings I gave the bar tender some cash for the damage I caused.

The penitent buys jewelry and runs for his life

Atonement! In addition, I bought several pieces of shit jewelry at the beach from some sales women. In the belief of doing something good, to give these poor women, a little income for the day, I didn't expect their obtrusiveness. They wanted to get rid of their necklace, earrings, and all different kinds of jewelry. Due to off season it seemed I was the only tourist at the whole beach. The only victim! I saved myself by running into the water. Again, I ended in a beach bar, lucky me! Now it started to rain heavily – typical for this season. Fresh, fresh,   feeling relaxed, I soaked up several drinks, looking at the Incredible Indian Ocean, and I took birthday calls from overseas. A perfect day! It is always nice when your friends and family think of you, even when you pass by only from time to time because of collecting country points. In return, sending them postal cards and some notes and photographs via social media.

Goa Trance Music Club

But the day wasn't over yet. Party night ahead! Even though there was no full moon party's available coz of the rain season, there was still the Goa typical, techno-electro-dance, beat bars ready to blow the mind away. I crashed some of the ones close to the beach and was welcomed, just like that: "Everything that happens in Goa, stays in Goa" – The same line is waiting for you in Bahrain, the red light district of the middle east, or in Vegas baby!. In addition, the Goa sentence counts especially during the high season of December and January. They also say there: "Come in the

Season, fuck in the Season". No wonder why so many Russian bears, English conquerors and Australian Backpackers travel to Goa. Never mind if it's the peak, or rainy season: You will always find the orgiastic trance highlights on da dancefloor!

Colorful mix for Indulgement

"A bit more cucumber" - An advertisement line from a nineties German TV commercial comes to the drunken mind when thinking of indulgent India. Dining on the one side, massages on the other, with lots of wellness treatments – yeah that's the reason for coming to India. If it rains all the day your time can be spent relaxing in spas finding the pathway to heaven and down again. In opposition to Thailand, in India men only massage men and women only massage women. Happy Endings – rather not! Of course if you are hetero. Two days for the big cities should be ok. The huge distances can be covered best with trains, cars, or busses. For the adventure feeling, people can hire Tuk Tuks. The landscape is unique, and the people are very talkative. Open minded travelers find easily someone to share a drink, a meal, a bed. It's quite easy since India hosts up to 100 different languages. Aside of the culture and sightseeing, party life in Goa is a must. Best go in December, to flee from the cold European winters.

Three continents in three weeks

After the extended birthday weekend in India, the first summer trip was coming up. 2, 3 weeks – that's the plan. Depending on my assessment of country, interest, and value, rather long or short stays. Therefore, 1 night in Istanbul – family visit. That should be enough. Take a connecting flight to Germany for a Meeting with old friends for another day. One day lay over's in Estonia, Finland and Sweden. Bam. Bam. Bam. Focus on Argentina, Brazil, and Portugal. But also spending 3 days in each I didn't want to overstay there as well.

Istanbul – Home sweet home

Yallah! Let's go! Istanbul. Orient meets occident. Old meets new. Bla. Bla. Bla. Old meets new: Its everywhere in the world. Nevertheless I love this city. Friendliness of the Turks, the cleaned language by Mustafa Kemal in 1923, lots of delicious food aside of the German style "Doener mit allem – Doener with everything', the speed, the noise, simply everything. I cannot figure out if I had a crash with a girl, or purely with this city. This time a short visit with my sister, nothing wild, only 1 night. Situation update! Family bonding! I knew the city from former love affairs on and off. Best Boerek: in Beshiktas, Kumpir – Veggie filled big potato in Ortakoey. For romance lovers, the Maiden Island is the place to be. The Galata tower offers a great view above the city. European style – Just head to the French Quarter. Relaxing pub hopping and easy food loving shopping starting at Taksim square and walking down Istikal Street. In addition: Blue Mosque, Hagia Sofia, Topkapi palace, Bosporus and so on. Unforgettable the tiger milk, the so called Raki Schnapps best served after heavy meal. Alright! Been there, seen that, done that. Check!

Berlin - Airborne

Already in the plane to Berlin! Mama is calling, but also the friends. Souvenirs for everyone. Meeting in kind of Skybar: „Solar". Highlight: 14th floor chic restaurant with better dining. One floor above a cool bar. Great view above the skyline. Best place for first date. Or for the second. Light is dimmed, bar equipped with several swings, descent music. Stories and kisses can be exchanged easily.

Tallinn – German like city with Russian sound

Then off to Tallinn. On the central square of the capital it looks like the Alter Market in German city of Cologne, nearly identical. Oh, I could have stayed home instead. But a country point is a country point. The German knights have left their foot print here several centuries ago I guess. The only difference: In Estonia Russian is wider spoken than in Germany and in Cologne in particular. The local language is present too, but sounds more like finish. Aside of the obligated sightseeing tour – with a rickshaw bicycle driver there was the need to try the local drink: Vodka of course, since the country is close to the motherland of this little water – literally translated. Luckily I stayed only 1 night since there wasn't much to see or do that I couldn't do somewhere else in Europe. In addition, I needed to keep my power for being ready for the next day's finish wedding of my friend's outside Helsinki.

Power wedding play in Helsinki

By ferry, it takes only 2 hours from Tallinn to Helsinki. The plan: Quick hotel check in, a power workout followed by a power nap, and a rapid rush into party readiness status for the wedding. Nada! Niente! Even in Radisson Blu hotel check in is only after 2pm. Really? Only via upgrade against some extra money, early check-in is possible. Money talks and opens doors!

Finish drinkers and wedding speeches

There are drinking nations such as Germany, England, Russia, and Ireland. Ha! Nearly forgotten the infamous Finns! Damn! How could I forget my Afghanistan mission years ago, where after only 4 months duty, 2 Nordic men had been sent home for their drunk service. Mission alcoholished! Oh, that was the reason why the party people had already prepared some flasks in their tuxedos, and already by 3pm at the coffee and cake buffet, the "Finlandia Vodka" was ready to be killed. No wonder that only 2 hours later half of the crowd had already some drinks in their blood. Logically, I started my wedding speech like this: "Hey lovely friends from Finland! You are drunk. I am drunk! Because of that I keep it short and I leave the finish translation out." The guests who laughed and applauded seemed very pleased. Of course, they just wanted to continue drinking. The Finns are good in ski jumping, fast driving and drinking as it seems. Alright: "Kippes – Cheers!" were my last words of the speech. Once my Russian teacher said: "You learn a foreign language on the pillow of your girlfriend, or while drinking."

Make it here, make it there – best is we make it anywhere

Two or three Vodkas later, a Finnish surprise made her way onto the dance floor. A local one, who wanted just more than holding hands. Problem: Not only with her kid and husband on the party – I was worried about the German image and my safety. Do I want to risk that! I will be massacred by a Finnish giant and we Germans are the bad conquerors again? No! We need to avoid this! Not again. We lost already in World Wars. But there, I didn't expect the finish counter offence. I couldn't even let it go by trying to slow her down by mentioning the missing suitable location. Her hotel room? Husband alarm! Ergo: No! Ladies toilet! Men's room? Hm. In my head: Both were maybe filled with guests, then, when I looked up and saw the wheelchair sign! That's it! Great! No one is there anyway, and it is more spacious. That's the plan. A man has to do what a man has to do. It's in the genes. Stupid! It's in the history as well. Germany again on blitzkrieg mode.

Alcohol is always the solution

Until then, I had survived without any accidents. But embarrassment didn't wait long for me. The husband of the finish lady wanted to offer me a drink later on. Not because of my German – Finish liaisons but because I was a good fellow and guest. Maybe he was mistaken. I didn't feel well. Even a German can have feelings. But I was too drunk to start some kind of clarifications about sense and non-sense of life.

Stockholm – Swedish for Berlin

On the next morning another ferry was waiting, this time to Stockholm, a city that looks like Berlin. The only difference: People are more blonde, taller, speak another language and the water in the canals and bays is salty. The city is pretty flat plus has nice royal ancient buildings – such as Berlin. Could be a good spot to run a marathon in the future. Maybe awesome fast times could be possible as well. Other touristic highlights are: Vasa Museum about the Swedish history, roof walk sightseeing tour, Ice bar where you get – 20 degrees Celsius atmosphere and vodka shot glasses made of real ice. Enough action for 1 day!

Hotel Mama in Lisbon

Next stop the capital of Portugal. There I made a home stay for 3 nights as the guest of an older couple. The good lady I knew from Saudi Arabia – former colleague. Once she said whenever one of us would travel to Portugal we could stop by for a coffee. I took this little finger offer and grabbed the whole hand by staying at their place completely. I felt like home since I didn't pay anything for accommodation or for any meal. Even, I got the luxury that they drove me around Lisbon, showed me the beaches, and organized sightseeing trips to the Casino place Estoril, cultural spots such as Cascaise.

Port wine love affair

But the best was the introduction of Port wine. It's a more sweet tasty wine, to be drunk after a meal. But once you have fallen in love with this red dream fluid you can have it all day long. Nevertheless I tried to invite my hosts several times to dinner to say thank you for their great hospitality – but no chance. The only disadvantage when staying at friends places you need to be home on time. Similar to hotel mama! Meaning: Party time in Lisbon wasn't possible this way. But having relaxing moments and a timeout once in a while could be good as well.

Brazilian fake nudes

Oh my goodness! The entire world is talking about the bikini beauties of the Copacabana. Or the girls from Ipanema. No way Jose! Totally overrated. 4 days in Rio and Sao Paolo showed the women potential is not even among the top 10 in the world. Chauvi police alarm! Alright on TV when the carnival is on and when all different kinds of girls from all over Brazil will be deported to Rio the people abroad melt when they see these ladies. After hours of makeup work and when we dream about Brazilian football and cocktails we believe these women are female gods. In reality: Total failure! Total disappointment. When you travel to different places in the world and make your assessment in the afternoon at 3pm during the week the ladies, and partly the men, are much better in Ethiopia, Belarus, Ukraine, France, Italy, Lebanon, Japan, Thailand and Peru. There you can find better wedding material than in Brazil. For granted! Period! At least the men can play soccer. 5 times world champions – that's the fact. One word only: Pele. Enough said. And not to be forgotten: Caipirinha. One of the best drinks ever. Similar impact to Scottish Whiskey, Pisco Sour of Peru, German Beer, Russian Vodka, or Sake from Japan.

Buenos Aires – Hot spot de la Tango

Three nights in Argentina, the home of Maradona. My childhood hero. For "Pele" I was born too late. First Soccer World Champs: 1986. Mexico mi amor! There Diego won the title nearly alone! He is nearly a soccer god. The Gauchos have founded a religion after him. That was the reason to visit also the stadium where he played, including the Boca Juniors soccer museum. In addition I had on the agenda: Tango show, Wine tasting and Argentinian steak. 3 days should be enough.

Water side steak treatment

On arrival having a walk down to the harbor and entering a beautiful restaurant and sampling Vino tinto marsh and Steak Vamos Muchacho was a treat! We are in Argentina. Short night, only because of a planned early morning sightseeing bus trip, also tired from walking in my shoes. For developed, relatively safe cities a combination of Hop on – hop off bus tours with a sightseeing walk is the best for cost – benefit ratio. First, for getting an easy overview of the city and second, deepening my knowledge on the points of interest.

Hoppla hop into the bed of heaven

After the morning foot march through the Argentinean capital I lacked sugar intake. Flat! K.O.! Hungerast – the German favorite world of Tour de France champ Jan Ullrich. Therefore I went quickly into a cafe around the corner and took reinforcement via carbohydrate intake plus a caffeine load. At the same time, I checked a map of the surrounding area and made a battle plan for further day's activities. Promptly, I could catch the look of a nice blonde over my right shoulder. She seemed interested in what that strange guy is doing with old fashioned maps. My touristic taxi ride espanol helped me to make the first contact, and after the quick fact checking, I had to do some arrangements for dinner that night. If the lady is happy about the dinner she would join some cocktails in a bar of my "tourist to do list" of Buenos Aires. So it went. With the motivation of Indulgence of food and drinks satisfied, the mutual taxi drive ended at my hotel. 4 stars double room is usually better than an 8 peeps hostel room, when engaging with a lady while travelling. It seems when I travel solo I am never alone.

Cross country in Uruguay

On the next morning, the Senorita kicked me out of my own bed, saying I need to get my extra country point. Now I could remember that I told her about my ambitious plan to do a day tour to the neighboring country of Uruguay. "Hey Muchacho, the ferry isn't waiting", more time cuddling was not possible. Off to the next country. After some hours on the boat I arrived in a kind of Mexican border town. At least I thought so when I saw the easy peasy stylish houses. I rented a buggy and drove 2 hours cross country. But I had to pay attention, coz I am the god of orientation. NOT! Without GPS I am lost. Even in Riyadh I go to work by using the navigation system. Safety first!

Senorita for second round

Late afternoon I was back in Buenos Aires. Tango Show! Per couple, and table, there was a vino tinto bottle! Lucky me! Senorita didn't want to join coz: Been there, seen that, done that. The whole bottle of red wine just for me. Tops! I am the winner! But here I couldn't finish the race. After 80 % I gave up. Wasn't in that great drinking shape or better: the cut off time was over since the restaurant and the real tango presentation were in 2 different locations and we had to move! In this transition process I crashed into another caliente lady – this time from Portugal. She seemed to be impressed by my travel stories, and click clack the eyes clapped. Like in a 90ies TV I had to make the decision now for the last night in BA. A Portuguese new entry or the senorita from last night. Better safe than sorry! Back to 4stars hotel and trusting the force of the first night. For future trips a safe harbor is set – even although I was not a sailor.

Paris – Mon amour

Return flight to good old Europe! My first time ever to Paris. City of love! Alone? No way! Meeting arranged with an old friend from school. Lunch with baguette, wine, and cheese under the Eifel tower at the river of Seine. That's the plan. Very romantic! Great! But from England the rain came over the channel and Plan B came into play. French café around the corner – just the second best solution. It was just alright. I told her about my Paris sightseeing so far: Eiffel tower, Seine, bus tour, louvre, etc. I always thought the tower looks like the radio tower in Berlin, or the television tower of Tokyo in Japan. But the entire world creates mega hype for it. Nevertheless when I checked my photographs later on – every second one showed the tower. Strange! If in Paris you cannot live without it.

Trading under the Eiffel tower

The dinner was really expensive. Like so many things in the French capital. Even a normal coffee costs up to 8 Euro. Really heartbreaking were the cheap souvenirs. Under the Eiffel one guy sold 5 mini towers for all together 1 Euro. I gave him the recommendation to ask for higher prices to make a better deal but he misunderstood and gave me another additional one on top. I guess my French wasn't that great – same as his English. However my friends and colleagues at home are always happy about the souvenirs I bring to them from all over the world. That makes them happy, as well as me. Terrific!

Better saving than sorry

This trip was great. Air plane ticket Stockholm – Lisbon – Sao Paolo – Paris for just 1000 Euro. Nearly every second stay was a home stay with friends. Couchsurfing is calling. Also for free, plus new contacts. That's the future. In addition: If the conquered lady is in for a restaurant to 80%, she will be also joining the after session in a by 80 %. Mutual bedside stories included for further 80%. I guess for female single travelers there should be a similar ratio. However I heard a story about a book writer that aimed for travelling in 80 women around the planet. But he fell in love with number 20 or so and had to stop apparently. Good plan – bad conclusion. Maybe he is not a good finisher.

Triple Trip to down under

By now I have been to all continents except Australia and Antarctica. Therefore I wanted finally to go down under. Best to do it in combination with New Zealand. Due to cheap air fares, and my flexibility I booked a return flight to Nepal, followed by a triangle ticket from Kathmandu via Sydney to Kiwi land.

On the roof of the world

Kathmandu – The capital of Nepal the mountain country is full mystical spirits: Base camp, high altitude sickness, frozen toes, spirituality, hiking, trekking, bungee jumping, food poisoning, and yoga – the range of key words is long when I made my pre- research before the trip. Nevertheless I looked forward to this trip – bringing me to higher states and levels in any ways.

German angst doesn't jump

On arrival I got the impression to be at the beginning of life itself. I believed to travel to Kathmandu also naked. Then you can buy at nearly every corner backpacks from all different brands as well trekking clothes. In addition there are so many opportunities to travel via bus. Schedules were all over the place to nearly every Asian destination. In parallel there are shops also offering a Visa for these destinations. But I had only 3 days and I wanted to book some tours for hiking, a flight to Mount Everest, and wild water rafting. For bungee jumping and other adventures I am not the guy. Rather I travel to dangerous countries than jumping out of a plane or having my life depending on a rubber band. Don't like to lose the control. Ok. I could also say I didn't have time. Sounds manlier as an excuse.

On the pathway to heaven

The hiking with the pack was very amusing. Nearly 8 hours up and down with light showers passing happy smiling people. There I recognized: Never mind if it is 40 degrees plus or minus – the Nepalese guy has always a little heat on plus weather – water proofed face, light brownish and always smiling. And they have a kind of shining: A mystic – Buddhist – peaceful charity atmosphere. Not only their hearts are open as well their houses. That's the reason why so many backpackers on short budget travel to this little country. In Nepal you can find the travel world. No wonder why it's so crowded there – especially when climbing up Mount Everest. Easy to spot: Mostly females that didn't serve in the army before trying "heavily packed" to go on a hike or to find new mental heights in one of the Buddha yoga treatment temples. Especially for the hiking or trekking part in each army of the world you get paid for it and don't need to do it in your vacation again. Since you have to carry armor, a weapon, and take responsibility for your subordinates. Ok mostly army hiking takes place in war zones where people try to kill you proactively.

Nepal – The best country of the world - sadly without beach access

If it had a beach Nepal would easily be one of the top 5 travel countries among the 200listed. Nowhere else can you find such friendly people, a cultural diversity, from local Buddhist spirit to international globetrotters, food delights, cheap travel costs, close distance to god (whichever one you believe in), military elite (Gurkhas) and A1 clothing (Kashmir shawls). In addition, a splendid landscape with proactive vacation adventure opportunities. All that is surrounded by the sound of Shangri-La sounds, car horns, and a mix of different languages, between Anglo-American-Latin-Indo-Germanic to Mandarin-Hindi-Nepalese.

Road site omelet deluxe

The first thing that comes to mind when a backpacker arrives in a Nepalese hostel is not the question about food, or electricity – it's about hot water. Mostly you can dream of Wi-Fi. But if that is sorted the rest comes along such as the best food in easy conditions. On a morning reconnaissance for a breakfast place in Kathmandu I discovered the best food in the world: 1 Dollar omelet wrapped in an old newspaper. I had before all different kind of meals when travelling from 5 Stars to pish quality. But this one was unique and very tasty. This omelet beats it all. The price in combination with the ambience was awesome.

Swiss sweet heart for Kathmandu

After my trip to Nepal I met Christian from Switzerland that heart beats even more for Nepal than mine. He actually travels regularly to Kathmandu since he is supporting the Shanti Sewa Griha Center, a hospital which supports people suffering from leprosy, handicapped children and also a school for children of people in need. "There is still a great need for help, but together we can make a difference!" Christian is sure about it. In moments like that I feel kind of bad when rushing through countries, spending cash for just ticking off countries. Maybe in future I can be so generous like him. But first travelling more.

Sydney City surf paradise

Continue to Australia. Bondi or Manley Beach – Never mind any dream beach is a good beach. And if you are in Australia a surf lesson is a "must to do", especially when you come from a provincial village town in East Germany without any beach nearby. In a similar style, like the "Baywatch" safety guards the surf teachers of Sydney look like: Long blond curly hair, sunbathed skin, muscles all over and six-pack of course. A surf teacher without a six-pack is not a surf teacher. In addition, it seems like that all teens of the Anglo-Americans hemisphere fly down under to party all day. Drink-Party-Surf-and Bang! offers in hostels, crashes on drinks, both genders and all sophisticated values. Drink orgies – the connection of the western decadence. Carnival of Cologne or Octoberfest style at the beach with surfboards – that's Australian party life.

Mordor is calling in New Zealand

Canada is the better America (better English, more cultural, somehow more grounded), Switzerland (richer, sexy German language, sophisticated) is the better Germany and New Zealand the better Australia. They have got hobbit town, the volcanoes, super lakes, bungee jumping, white water rafting and skydiving – all seems possible. The northern island around Taupo made the heart beat higher. Unique!

A region far, far away

The best of this trip: Great cost-benefit ratio. 1000 Euros for a Middle East return trip to Kathmandu and a Triangle booking of Kathmandu – Sydney –

Auckland – Kathmandu. With prices like that it's an obligation to book a flight and conquer the tourist world. Collecting country points made easy and cheap. Nevertheless: Bring Australia and New Zealand closer to Europe and the level of beauty would be lower. Usually things in life are more attractive if they are far, far away. That's the reason why the paradise is not easy to reach as well. Or?

Doha for NYE

Even before coming to Saudi Arabia I always tried to spend NYE in a different country. Not necessarily new country at all but new for NYE. The closure of each year stays better in your mind! Unforgettable! Already done: Amsterdam (Love, peace, and rock n roll), Istanbul (Full power doner Kebab), Prizren (Army mission possible), Warsaw (Your German car is already there) and last year Riyadh (Calling for oil). This year Doha, the capital city of Qatar. Little party with friends. Nothing wild, but a new NYE country celebration point and reconnaissance for soccer world cup 2022.

2012 – Latin Love with Putin

Japan - The perfect nation

South Korea and Japan in a double trouble pack, right at the start of 2012. Quickly I discovered that the Japanese are the Germans of Asia. Not only was there the alliance with the Germans in World War 2, they both have a similar mentality (Asia for the Asians equals the Japanese). Plus obviously they didn't make friends when conquering their neighbors – such as the Germans. Since then they are critically looked at from all countries nearby. But there are further similarities: They also can build cars, and they are on time and tidy. Delays of the trains are measured in seconds. On train stations there are markers even advising where the guests have to wait when the trains are approaching.

Rich culture is not for free

The Japanese have got a rich culture, their own sports such as Karate, Judo, Kendo, Sumi, Aikido etc. The food is also popular worldwide. Yeah! there is more than just Sushi and Sake. Surplus on the streets: The superb beauty of the Thai's, well organized public transport like in Singapore, drinking like the Russians, perfection like Suisse made watches, creative like the artist in Berlin but driving on the left side. Yes – that's the Japanese mix of success. But you cannot get these advantages for free. As a tourist you have to pay a high price. Aside of Iceland, Djibouti in Africa and Switzerland – Japan is one of the most expensive countries. My indicators for that are either a McDonald's burger or souvenirs. Beer bottle taps cost around 5 Dollars. The price isn't nice.

Bud heat due to warmed toilet seat

I travelled to Japan in winter time and noted that the Japanese ladies presented their "hot legs" with short skirts even when temperatures fall just below the freezing point. Another hot Japanese item: The toilet seats. In no other country there is such a rich toilet culture. Water flush, air blower in different levels of strength and angle. A paradise for bud lovers. LOL. Another hot and surprising thing: The little coffee cans out of automats. You can find them all over Tokyo. In winter you can warm your hands either by hot coffee, or hot Japanese legs. Depending on confirmation by the ladies of course.

Speed up your travel life

In Africa some movements can take several days to make it between A and B in comparison to the Japanese who have their speed trains "the Shinkansen" on which the tourist can travel through time and space quickly. The passing landscape is great. The ride itself it is not spectacular in comparisons to German speed trains because in there are no complaining Germans, no delays, no non-working ACs and no unfriendly stewards.

World War II tour through Europe

A party in France while trying to reach Moscow and ending up in Italy – similar to the German Army campaign in WW II. In memory of historic moments one week in June should be spectacular to tick off of some new countries, and having fun as well. Even in speed mode.

Beach party a la francaise

Kick off for this week's trip should be France to attend a beach wedding. My best study buddy wanted to say "Qui Cherie" to his French lady in the south of France. Romantic! Beautiful! Party celebration of the German – French love at the beach of Cap d Agde! Nobles pure! 3 days in a row on a high level. On Friday: meeting with all family members to get to know each other, with the help of French Wine. I combined this trip with the new country point of Monaco. 4 hours layover should be enough for 2 nice pictures with yachts and Ferraris including a glass of champagne to celebrate! In addition, having a nice talk about soccer with a Dutch couple about the ongoing European Championship. Always fun playing soccer with the Dutch and talking as well. From German perspective of course.

Chardonnay breaks the ice

Away from Monaco heading west with 2 hours delay by train passing stunning beaches and bays. Off to the wedding party spot to meet up with family, friends and colleagues. German, French and British - such as in the World War, but this time, all on one side to celebrate. Drinking French Wine, partying together, family and friends getting along with each other. Another highlight of the night: Quarter final of the European soccer championship.

Germany ruled here again and qualified for semifinal.

French at the beach

Before the real wedding party kicked off the next afternoon I headed towards the beach for a relaxing chill out. In addition, I pimped my wedding speech. German and English part done. But after one, two glasses Bordeaux Wine I added some lines, the French was reviewed by a charming French bartender. The evening could come. Allez le blue! Vive la friends!

James Bond gets them all

Again wedding time! Again black tuxedo! Again a wedding speech! Without much effort, another lady out of the audience came along. OMG. Either it is the 1000 US Dollar Tux looking like 007 after some drinks or the wedding speeches have always the right tone to make the ladies run after me. Most likely it's the alcohol and the party atmosphere, that make people come together. Simple!

Go east!

Wedding party until 4 am, Lights off. Shower on. Taxi march. Airport, ready to fly. Berlin Meeting with friends at Wannsee, a nice old German restaurant. Another short night! Mother Russia as a next new country was waiting. Go east!

Defeat at the Moscow Metro system

I felt ready for Russia: Got Russian friends, school knowledge of the language, studied the history of different battles. But on arrival I got lost in the translation by ordering a day pass for the metro system of Moscow. Nada, niente, nix verstehen. "Ja, ne ponimayo – I don't unterstand!". In 1941 the German troops also brought the only the metro system just 13 km outside Moscow to a halt. History repeats itself.

The blonde angel saves the day

The lady behind the ticket desk didn't understand my Russian at all – NOT! Hers was Alien to me as well. Suddenly like in movie there was this blonde angel next to me, the wonder woman of the day, early 20ies, beautiful! She spoke in her best Russian to me. I tried with English in return. Then she took my arm and wanted to know where was heading. Red Square, Lenin Mausoleum, and then the journey began. She ordered the right tickets and took me through the stunning metro system of Moscow for about 30 minutes with different stops and changes. Russian Gastfreundschaft. Always wondering that the Germans are welcomed in Russia even they brought lots of pain in the past. Maybe that is the deal: Past is past. Living now to create the future. However, her help was very surprising. But most welcomed!

With the 20 Dollar Putin on Facebook

When we arrived at red square the Russian president Putin was waiting already. Yeah baby! Correct. But there was Lenin and Stalin as well. Ah I see. All look a likes. Ok, quickly a photograph for the social media. Nix da. „20 Dollars! " Shouted Putin. „10? ', I tried. „No I am Putin. 20 Dollars." Ok, if he is Putin I want to believe it and pay the price. I The blonde Angel took my smartphone. In the typical world leader positions such as handshakes, waving to camera, and pointing with fingers to each other we had a lots of photo motives done. Ready for Facebook!

The vodka information desk

Afterwards, the typical shots: Selfie here, panorama there! Click, click, click! Now to organize a sightseeing bus tour. No information nearby! Bad! Best part: Heading into the next 5 Stars hotel to get the necessary information by a qualified bar tender. When in a Russian bar I wanted to use this opportunity to tick off the travel obligation of having a local drink. The national one in Russia: Vodka. The bartender gave me a tablet PC and scrolled around 2 minutes through maybe more than 200 Vodka types. After two Vodkas on the rocks he gave me the tip to go to the central station to check out sightseeing busses. Well! We will see and ride.

Vodka connecting people

Walking in my tired shoes to the station. It was Big! So many people! But I couldn't spot any bus company; instead, I stood in front of a ticket automat. Lots of Russian destinations. A friendly Russian guy helped me out and asked me where I wanna go. Sightseeing in Moscow and maybe St. Petersburg. Yes, the former capital of the Russian Empire. Quickly he booked a return ticket for me. Not for the bus, but for the train. Part of the Trans-Siberian railway! Departing in 30 minutes. Without any luggage and not really ready I thought: "Go with the flow". Together with a Russian family, some beer and Vodka I started this little overnight trip. Quickly I improved my Russian due to alcohol and the friendliness of the Russians. "Nastarowje!" – Cheers. German – Russian friendship. It seemed there is no big world politic in this train car. As long the alcohol is running the world peace is safe. Could be an option for today's global leaders to prevent crisis and wars. Drinking together! Make love and party, not war!

No Power no photographs

Sunrise! Arrival after what seemed a short night without a descent sleep. Tourist bus booked immediately including a sightseeing boat trip. Without a proper coffee I overslept nearly the whole bus tour and wasn't able to do photographs. My bad luck and such a pity in that great beautiful city. Next try: Boat tour, but sadly here as well, I slept like an angel, mostly due to the waves of the water.

Nevertheless I bought some souvenirs for the people at home.

A Russian bar without Vodka is not a Russian bar

Highlight at Moscow airport. To make some more friends and by expressing my euphoria about the next country point I intended to invite to 2 Russian guys at a bar for a vodka. Big failure! All drinks possible but the Russian national one. Really? „A Russian bar without Vodka is not a Russian bar", I thought and ordered 3 beers. However! Nastarowje and prost!

German victory in Moscow 2018?

Usually at airports I have a lot of time to reflect on my current trip, plan ahead and make a lessons learnt study. Here, I recognized after 3 days travelling in Russia that the people don't smile very often but seemingly they can be very happy – especially when drinking vodka. In comparison the people from Thailand smile nearly all the time even they are not always happy – especially when there is another military coup on the way. For the near future it came to my mind if it's possible for the Germans finally to win in Moscow after their defeat in WW II. 2018 is the Soccer world championship. There are already different headlines reflecting the history.

Vatican swing with Ragazzi

From Moscow via Berlin to Bella Roma with the Irish Ryan Air machine. The airplane was full of Italians. No wonder, nearly at the same time as the flight took off there was the German kick off against Italy at the European football Championship. At the start of the game Italy was leading by 1 goal. OMG! Touchdown after 2 hours. Same for the Germans, Lost again! English soccer hero Gary Lineker once said: "Soccer is a game of 22 people hunting a ball and at the end Germany always wins." That might be true. But another truth is, Germany and Italy played for centuries and Germany cannot win – at least in big tournaments. Again on this occasion. The Squadra Azzuri went to the final. Despite of the Italian fans being crazy on the streets of Roma it was a great night with awesome sightseeing and the sky full of stars, no clouds, the moon was shining and the red – white – green flags all over the place. Met my Lebanese buddy from Beirut times at the central station. Immediately, we passed the victory drunken Tifosi going directly to the Vatican Security fence. Never mind taking a swing and country point saved. Great Effort! Enough! To top it off a photograph with three Roma ladies.

Dress to impress

This trip showed that for wedding parties no need for a hotel room. Either staying with a conquered wedding beauty, party through the night or sleeping and passing out on the dance floor. To get a "free ladies" accommodation for this night men have to be dressed better than the groom. That works easily when married in the past and the tux is still fitting. For women it works accordingly. Ok. It's hard to look better as the bride but at each wedding there is minimum one lady in red that has got a similar high attention rate by the crowd as the bride.

Latin Lovers in Lima

Shortly after in July I was off to South America, to include among other countries Columbia, Ecuador, Chile, Bolivia and Peru. With a landing at 1 am in Peru I expected to go for a whole night of Salsa dancing with a hot Latina. All was set! Flight booked! Communication done! Confirmation received. Thought the fire of love could be set. OMG! Naivety has a new name! 1 hour delay in arrival. Communication in Taxi driver espanol and IPhone 3 quality at the airport was not great. When I called Muchacha there was no direct Si or Nao. Typically for ladies in this country? No clue. However I felt the night would go in a different direction than planned.

Catching the birds with the right wingman

Finally, I arrived at the little hotel in the heart of Lima, capital of Peru. In the lobby I recognized a young Chico and shouted immediately: "Hey dude, can you speak Spanish AND English, si? Comprende?" Luckily he did and he asked the senorita at the phone if she is in for hot dancing and more this night. Obviously not! Flexibility is the basic skill when travelling. So I changed the plan and took the Chico as a wingman for partying in the clubs of the city. Since he was Chilean he knew how to talk. He did a good job so we rapidly had 2 ladies with us for the night. Logically the night was short and intense. For the next day's the company was set since we had further arrangements with them planned. That's America del sur! Vamos!

Hit and run in South America

Peru was on this trip the focus with Pisco Sour (local cocktail), Machu Pichu sight training (one arm pushups), and Guinea pig for lunch. Bolivia: Camera stolen out of luggage. Columbia: Survival of the fittest (some people say: "For Bogota one day is enough to get shot") and having some Salsa lessons in the Capital of this dance in Cali. Ecuador: Up to the mountain of Cotopaxi with 2 local ladies (what else) and finally meeting the old Chilean wingman from Peru in Santiago de Chile for his Birthday party again. And before flying out quickly up into the Andes for a skiing lesson. Nearly 2 weeks for this trip. Again a hit and run tour.

Obstacle road trip in South Africa

October, 2 months later, another 5 days off. To bridge it with the weekends at the beginning and the end means a possible 9 to 10 travel days. With proper planning I could travel through 4 new countries, especially in Europe, it could be possible.

But this time it was Africa, for years I wanted to do a road trip there. South Africa was the place to be and to do such an adventure. To be on the safe side, best to be travelling with friends to help out when having a flat tire or any other technical issue with the car. I started proactively looking for company on my trips since it got a bit boring travelling alone. Always sharing fresh information via Facebook is good but not that non-plus ultra. If you want to have a beer with a friend social media doesn't offer that service (yet).

However, I expected fun, excitement and discussion when travelling with my Texan mate, German Kris and a South African Lady friend. Even with delays we could use the good roads to cover 4 countries. How? Easy! Lesotho is completely surrounded by South Africa and partly Swaziland. Plus: Mozambique is north-eastern country bordering South Africa. Originally my plan was flying in to Johannesburg, renting a 4 wheel drive and crossing Lesotho slowly via the challenging Sani Pass, but full of adventures and a great landscape. After a left turn through Swaziland we made a short visit in Maputo the capital of Mozambique, finishing again in Johannesburg. 10 days of a wild Jeep ride up and down. Short but intensive!

Multi-interest sightseeing tour

After asking several people to join this ride, my trio infernal came across and the plan changed. That's the thing by travelling with other people: Compromises. I said: "We can all do different things, I don't care. The only thing is to cover all 4 countries". All of my three friends wanted to see the beautiful Cape town in the Southwest, in Durban (South East) surfing and partying in Johannesburg (short: Joburg). Ok. Well! I made the plan for all their wishes. New plan: Flight Riyadh to Joburg and connecting flight to Cape Town. Then by rental car, travel via Bloemfontein heading east. Breakfast in Lesotho, onto Durban, passing Swaziland and one night in Maputo.

Face to face with the great white

After Texas Clint nearly smashed the gears of our vehicle coz of riding in 3rd gear for hours (maybe he believed it was an automatic car such as these in USA), we got our second excitement: Facing real sharks. Southeast of Gansbay we booked cage diving with the big white. We believed that could bring more action than a helicopter ride. Well, well, well! Great decision! The boat captain teased the dangerous sharks with bloody meat. All of us got their advantages: The sharks got lots to eat and the tourist great photographs. The sharks came really close. Face to face, or better, nearly nose to nose. Without the cage the killers could have taken the tourists as an extra appetite bit. Strangely I didn't have any anxious feeling. I was only concerned about getting the best pic under the water. But when I checked the shots later with the rows of teeth and the wide open mouth I got strange feelings anyways.

Breakfast police stop in Lesotho

After South African Dinner show, a harbor sightseeing tour and spotting the table mountain in the distance, go east! Breakfast in Lesotho. 2 hours in this tiny country! That was the plan. The border crossing went strangely rapidly with the car. After the small breakfast when exiting the country we quickly recognized the reason: We missed the entrance stamp. The border guard officer in charge checked this issue and questioned us in her office. We tried to convince her that was just a mistake and we didn't intend to enter her beautiful country illegally. We said they just waved us through when entering. But the officer didn't want to believe that.

Quickly it became emotional. Words became louder and louder. But Master Kris could calm her down with his charming words and smiles. Otherwise we wouldn't have any chance. We were nearly out of her office when our female South African leady wanted to restart with the arguing. A real catfight was on the horizon. As far as I can remember I whispered into her ears to "shut up" coz we are nearly out. My backup would have been to kiss her and to pull her out of the office to make her silent. Easy: When you are kissing you cannot complain.

Law and order in Swaziland

Further ride through Swaziland. Easy peasy! Big mistake! Coming from South Africa into Swaziland was quite ok. This time we paid attention to get all the stamps. Check! All good! But after passing through for couple of hours and then when we wanted to leave Swaziland, the border police officer made trouble. He wanted to see different papers. This time I directly went offensive and ask him concerning how much money he wants to get bribed with. Failure again! He just wanted to get some extra documents for the car. We didn't have all necessary permissions. Our trip came to stop here at the border. I quickly calculated our space-time horizon if we had to go back we wouldn't be able to tick off country four (Mozambique) plus our outbound flight from Johannesburg would be hard to catch. No way, Jose! Luckily we found a little place with a phone and fax machine at this border post. All was not looking promising. Center of Africa with wild animals and we were the only, somehow, good dressed whites there. No one gave us a smile. We didn't feel well at all. I didn't expect a successful outcome of calling our rental car service in Cape Town and getting promptly a fax back to. But well, it's the African way, they say. All went surprisingly fast and effective. Great! Sometimes it is good to throw away negative thinking and prejudices and be open minded and hopeful. At the end we could manage also this border crossing point. Top!

Three traffic tickets in one day in Mozambique

We got roller coaster feelings in Mozambique. In this former Portuguese colony there was a kind of Caribbean feeling coz of the Latin like language. I got a new personal record in traffic fines. Since I was the dedicated driver I got the honor to bring our big car onto a little shaking ferry boat with a big load of people. I believed half of Africa would be travelling with it. I had to adjust our parking position millimeter by millimeter to not hit or touch one of the thousand legs. After mastering that challenge I got a traffic ticket by cutting one corner, being a ghost rider and furthermore driving us into a road work station. But at the end we all survived also this incredible tour. 4 more countries under the belt but as well having ticked off lots of adventures.

2013 – From food poisoning to imprisonment

Western boys go crazy in South East Asia

At the beginning of this trip in Kuala Lumpur, the capital of Malaysia, together with some Arabic acquaintances I wanted to celebrate NYE in style. Add on: My Texas buddy wanted to join as well. Furthermore, we planned to tick off Cambodia and Brunei as well. Plus for me: Vietnam. But first the NYE party in the Skybar with the direct view to the Petronas towers.

Arabic party management vs. German impatience

After the warm up drinking session in the late afternoon / early evening of NYE we started heading towards the real party battle spot. I assumed my Arabic friends had organized a table or ticket or something like that for the Skybar. But alarm alarm! Nothing was done. Stupid me, I could have asked already on arrival but maybe I already had too much drinks. However, when in the taxi going to the party I recognized something could be wrong. Wild crowd of people! Quickly I calculated the time and the space in-between us and the party. Nothing good was the result. Somehow the movement was as slow as in No-man's-land on the western front in World War I. NYE without Texan buddy and without champagne – no way! That's no option! 20 Minutes to New Year! Where is Texas Clint? Where is the party? The clock is ticking and time running! In the hotel tower of the Skybar – too many people were lining up to get up to the Skybar. Waiting for the lift! Rumors made the round for the need of tickets. We should have been there already 2 hours ago. Oh man! Ok. German impatience is calling, German complaint policy as well. But wrong planning is wrong planning.

A sorrow shared is a sorrow halved

Finally! At least Master Clint was there now. Quick briefing to him: „Arabic organization. Nothing prepared. No tickets. Now off to next bar. I pay the champagne!" Definitely, I didn't want to spend the NYE with the other friends anymore and keep my moody mood. With Clint the sun was rising again. Even he didn't have army background but he rapidly recognized the serious situation. I guess because of his American – Texan roots. Like a cannonball we headed off down the road. 10 minutes to go to midnight. "There, a bar on left, or better, a restaurant on right?" Heart rate 180, 5 minutes left. I decided for the bar. Good choice.

All's well that ends well

The bartender was irritated when I immediately ordered a bottle of champagne without asking for the price. When you get 2 minutes left until midnight at NYE you cannot make long conversations. 4,3,2,1 – Prost – Cheers! Hallejullah and Happy New Year! With Ami buddy, bubbly, firework and the PETRONAS towers in the back and standing at cocktail table at the poolside bar – off to a New Year. Due to my impatience I could save the NYE night. Terrific!

Dreaming in the rain of Halong bay

Already, after 4 hours of sleep riding in the taxi to the airport, I was off to Vietnam, without Clint. No visa issued. On arrival directly picked up by a travel group. I had pre-arranged a day trip to use the limited time from Airport to Halong bay and hotel check-in late at night. Unluckily, the sky was full of clouds with light rain. Sunshine would have been better of course. The atmosphere reminded me of Thailand, with all the small bays. Later in the day I arrived at the hotel. For night out activities I felt too tired. My body still was suffering from the NYE drinking event. And without pushing wingman the air was out of the balloon, and getting paid lady service was not my intention anyways.

Early morning flight from Hanoi to Hue, with a10 hours stay over. A quick taxi sightseeing trip to see special spots and taking some photo shoots. Via train, heading south to Ho Chi Minh City, and further on to Cambodia.

Phnom Penh – Shoot em like in Texas

I used the so called chicken bus, from Vietnam to Phnom Penh, Cambodia. There meeting again with Texas Clint. On the agenda: Shooting, party, sightseeing. Typical Texas style. One night spent in the capital of Cambodia, followed by Siam Reap, where the ruins of Angkor Wat are located. Most people know them from the Lara Croft movies. On arrival we quickly got ready for the day trip. After a quick shower we took a Tuk Tuk to a shooting hall. Since army times I haven't done bam, bam, bam.

Machine guns from different producers gave us fun for a half a day. Posing on old Russian army tanks and then off to get some drinks for the night.

Gangnam style on a bar table

Our tour led us from night bar to dance bar and so on until we reached several vodka Red Bull and met 8 local female beauties. The alcohol, the heat, the humidity and the travel fever helped us to get along with dancing. Texas Cowboy performed on the table the latest songs. Best: Gangnam style in Cambodia by a Texan. The female judges voted for the next round and 2 of them wanted to do an assessment of us in our hotel. Challenge: double room booked. Never mind the stage was ours.

Age beats the youngster

There was a German war movie in the 1990ies:"Stalingrad" where performance was related to the rank in the army. This time we decided that the mercy of early birth should be valued. So Texas man had to present his skills at the pool while Germany first ruled and showed his talents in the hotel room.

Poser plan leads to hospital

The next two days: Siam Reap. We travelled by boat killing some beers all the way and experienced the waterish landscape right and left of the river. Feeling free! My plan: One arm pushups recorded on video and uploaded to social media. Sometimes I do pushups in front of sightseeing spots worldwide to have another photo shoot aside of a selfie here, a selfie there. Usually, people, especially women, show always the same face, same pose. Boring! Only because of their sexiness, and the horny men watching they get thousands of likes and even get paid for it. Stupid! Jealous? Maybe! But it is also a kind of neutral assessment. It is a reflection of our time. And sex sold is always best. All the emancipated people in the world will shout out. But the likes in social media say the truth: Men have to be strong, successful, the hero. Women should be sexy, hot, and the princess. Period! Never mind this time photo / video shoot with the temples of Angkor wat in the background.

Water in – vomit out

Despite of all my ambitious plans: The stomach was calling. And these calls were not happy calls.

Indeed somewhere I must have caught something. Idiot me: Either salad on open buffet bar, or Gin Tonic on the rocks. Stupid! While travelling never use any of them. Even although my travel buddy consumed the same he was not having any symptoms. I had got severe food poisoning. The night before Siam Reap was spent on the toilet. All exits were open for release. Dehydration here we go. All water that came in went out immediately after. As well I showed an allergic reaction. My gum was swollen like hell. First I believed it's a kind of worm or whatever. In these moments I didn't think about pushups or visiting the sightseeing spots of Siam Reap. Help! All I need was help, and water, and a toilet. OMG!

Bed time Reggae

I was feeling awful the next day. Lips dry, totally dehydrated, no liquid in my mouth. Sleepy. weak. painful, Mama – help me! All I wanted: Visit of a doctor, getting medication, and rest. But in the little praxis I had to fill out a paper. "Man, where are we here? In Germany?" All that bureaucracy nonsense when I am nearly dead? All that came to my mind. But to get faster help I kept my mouth shut and followed the orders. Quickly put some cash onto the table. Relying on Insurance or other credit cards – I would be a dead man. Again: Cash of several hundred Dollars is always great. Finally, a doctor, medication, bed time. Day was over! Bam!

Texas nurse treatment

My Texas friend spent a great day at cultural heritage of Angkor Wat. He came home with a smile. Spontaneously, he turned into a male nurse and gave me all my necessary medicaments, tea, and butter bread. In such travel moments I was happy not being alone. The medicaments helped very well. So I could do a day tour on the next day. For the one arm push-ups I activated all my power. 10 seconds video shot done! Country mission accomplished.

How to visit a country

You consider you have visited a country only when you have been to hospital, at a wedding, having a love affair or being in prison. That's the credo from different travelers I met so far. In Kazakhstan I should face the imprisonment actually. Two months after the Cambodia experience I travelled to

Kazakhstan for sightseeing and watching a soccer world cup qualifier game from Germany. After a short 3 days home stay in neighboring Kirgizstan, which included kettle babysitting, horse riding, teaching judo in the wide grass fields of this former Soviet Union state, I needed to go back to Kazakhstan. I had booked a return flight from Saudi Arabia to Kazakhstan. And another return flight Kazakhstan to Kirgizstan to save money. Now on my way back via Kazakhstan to Riyadh. That was the plan. But I didn't plan it properly. I was not aware that there are multi reentry visa requirements also for other countries than Saudi Arabia.

Imprisonment in Kazakhstan

Around 10pm I reached the airport in Almaty and I was supposed to fly out again in the morning to the Middle East via Astana. The serious but friendly female officer told me I only had a single entrance visa and I need to return on next morning. Of course she could only speak Russian and not English. With my broken Russian I tried to tell her my intention just to have a stopover and actually want to visit her beautiful country again. I only wanted to go home and so I asked for a transit visa, but this wasn't possible. Bad luck! So I ended up in a 3 square meter cell together with a guy from Palestine. I calculated 2500 US Dollars extra flight costs plus 2 or 3 vacation days for the whole re-scheduled flight agenda. I tried to speak to my companion in this little prison and he actually wanted to give me recommendations on how to get out of this cell and get past immigration. But when he mentioned that he has been stranded there for almost 8 days I thought: "Hey man I don't think you are the best advisor for this topic!"

Free Wi-Fi saves the day and the way home

In my emergency situation I figured that the airport offers free Wi-Fi. Yippi! Quickly I checked flights to the Middle East for the next morning. After a short sleep and having fresh energy I tried all my travel charm with the new officer in charge. After the shift change there was another lady officer in place. I begged her by telling I only wanted to go home and flying out directly from this airport out of transit zone. She was more open to my ideas than the officer of last night. Great! I felt like I was in the movie "The last king of Scotland" or "Fargo" where people tried to escape from countries by using tricks and it took only seconds before they got caught!. After the green light of the lieutenant several other soldiers of immigration with lower ranks questioned me and checked the non-correct visa. Even I didn't need to fear for my life but when finally onboard I was so happy at having saved a lot of money and extra paid vacation days. I just didn't want to make a mistake while travelling. Nevertheless at this point of time I just had 78 countries visited.

Jet Ski power in Bahrain

Some weeks later I was off to neighboring Bahrain. Again this time it was party, party, party. In parallel to my travel hobby, organizing dinners in Riyadh for the Expat community is my pleasure. That's the way to meet new people, do business networking and having something else to do than only work. Soon I reached the point that I wanted more. So I started setting up little get-togethers, mostly in a chillier relaxing atmosphere to set off the day. Best time is at "sundowners" where the light, temperatures, and the whole atmosphere changes. Now I wanted to test this format abroad in Bahrain. I activated around 20 friends, colleagues and other peeps from Riyadh, Bahrain and UAE. Beach club march! 20 US Dollars entry fee should be ok. Live resident DJ, small beach bar, Jet skis for rent.

Agenda: 14.00 to 20.00 eating, drinking, Jet ski rids, sun burning and having a good time. Sun high in the sky, background skyline of Bahrain with skyscrapers, and hip-hop vibes. Women ratio 50%, In middle east it's very important. With some drinks in the blood people fly over the water by Jet Ski or dance to the music at the beach. Life is good with good company and sunshine!

Sundowner at its best

After several hours full power drinking and enjoying sunshine we slowly got tired. Same for the sun that went down and threw long shadows. Therefore a clever move: Taking the sun beds into the shallow water and turning them into the sundowner direction. Cold drink here, hot bodies there. Fun famous! Clearly there wasn't much going on this evening anymore. But hey party and fun shouldn't be only at night. The day has 24 hours available. It's clear that nothing much more happened this evening. The most of us were done. The alcohol and the heavy sun burned the heads away. Ok a little good night drink in a roof top bar had to be done anyways. But there we couldn't even increase the power by using Vodka – Red Bull. No wings made us fly. Shortly before 11 the lamps went off! Good night my lord!

Champagne brunch attack!

As regular early bird I couldn't sleep long and activated the companions. Off your beds buddies! Drink readiness march, march! Close to 10 already prepared for drinking at the hotel pool bar. Prost! Someone told us the night before there is a Radisson blu hotel offering champagne brunch for around 60 bucks open buffet all you can eat including champagne. That's sounded like a great deal. As a stingy East German fellow I needed to try this one. At least 2-3 drink buddies were up and running already and saw an added value in this brunch exercise. Taxi! here we go. Of course we had our luggage with us because of German planning and effectiveness we checked out before and wanted to hit the brunch and drinks followed by up and away back home via airplane. If you plan properly you can reach more in (travel) life: More countries, more fun, more drinks.

Eat, drink, and repeat!

On arrival the Radisson Blu, offered in the entrance hall was a big variety of food tables: Sushi, Indian,

Italian, Life cooking, Ice creams, deserts and, and, and! In Dubai, Abu Dhabi or in Bahrain: In bigger hotels there is on each Friday such all you can eat brunches, partly with bubbly and other spirits included. It is recommended to fast for 2-3 days to be able to get smashed on this Friday afternoon. It's a cool thing to meet friends, colleagues and other tourists for an eating and drinking event for more than 3-4 hours at descent prices.

Rapid refill rush

Yet even before the first glass could be emptied the next load was there already. In da background live music changed with an electro resident DJ. Add on, and very suitable: A descent pool with swim elements and floaty in ten meters distance next to the little dance floor stage. Champagne glass, flup, flup, into the hand and onto the air matrices. 35 degrees. Sunshine pure. Bam. That hit the brain. I even tried to do experiments to figure out the optimal filling for the glass: Preventing the glass from falling over and making it swim when I put it next to me into the water for swimming. Result: Between 30% and 70% glass load the glass is swimming perfectly without any support. In total such an afternoon is much better than the

Ballerman -parties on Mallorca since it is more cost effective. For a day at least. It's definitely a recommendation when visiting the Middle East.

Summer trip in the northern Hemisphere

Again nearly 3 weeks off work! But full on for country points! New ones scheduled for this trip: Ireland, Iceland, Canada, Cuba, Latvia and Lithuania. In addition, a stopover in Germany, Finland and the Territory of Greenland.

Light clothing in the heavy weather of Iceland

After short stop in Frankfurt continuing via Irish pub hopping, river dance shows, full Irish breakfasts and sightseeing tour I was off to Iceland. On arrival at night I saw lots of people with all kinds of backpacks and professional climbing gear. I felt like a little rookie and fully under dressed. This hiking and trekking community was well prepared for walking on glaciers, abseiling into dead volcanoes, or even diving between the plates of North America and Europe. It seemed that all were geared up for mastering Mount Everest. My humble travel experiences based on city tours in jeans, button shirts and sometimes even suit jacket. Always looking a bit like being on a business trip. My plan was to get quickly to the guest house, which I booked via hostelbookers.com and then have a nice good night's sleep.

Waiting in the rain of Reykjavik

From the airport we drove with all other backpackers and adventure guys to a kind of central square. It rained cats and dogs. My waterproof Gore-Tex jacket was well packed in my rucksack. Damn! When I left the transport bus also my motivation left – me! In the dark I didn't really know where to go. Already totally wet I hated this wet island. Especially because of the high costs for the 2 square meter room i had to pay 60 bucks. Luckily a local guy took me to the address of the house. Finally there I knocked the door and rang the bell. Nothing! What's that? In the middle of the night no one opened. „So eine Scheisse! – Such a shit! ". I called and the host wanted to be there in around 10 minutes. My goodness! Next time I will book a normal hotel with corresponding service. At least there was hot shower after.

Happy ending in the Blue Lagoon

The next three days I spent in cages, hiking in the rain and in overpriced bars. Other great adventures are: Diving between the American and the European continents, doing glacier walks and mountaineering. Some friends recommended me to eat whale and shark. Ok! Some lefty-vegan-animal lovers will complain now reading this but as a traveler that wants to experience nearly everything. Shark meat was served cold and t tasted very harsh. Really hard to say! The waiter recommended having these little shark bites with a little Schnapps. So I did take a local drink followed by the shark. Not bad! Shortly before my departure flight I went to the "Blue lagoon" - a thermal bath close to the airport. It's a magical point every visitor should indulge with nice drink in hand, some mud on the face and friends in the hot water. Impressive scenery enhanced with the mist, caused by the cold air temperature.

Greenland's hammer

When I told a friend I am going to Iceland he recommended that I book at least a day trip to

Greenland. It is not a country in that sense but an inhabited territory from Denmark. 400 Euro for a 2 hours flight, 4 hours sightseeing and 2 hours return. Not cheap but worth it. It reminded me of my Mount Everest flight passing in Nepal. Price and time was similar but was great as well. Already from the plane I could see all the beauty. The weather! God loved me on that day, clear blue sky. No cloud. Sunshine reggae. On arrival the air was so clear, ad together with the icebergs, the snow covered mountains, the crystal clear water and the blue sky – stunning! One of the best moments in my travel life. I guess when you grow up in a flat countryside without much snow, far away from a beach and not into skiing then this is really overwhelming. Great! Every penny well spent for this short trip! After visiting Greenland and Iceland I recognized that Iceland is green and Greenland is full of ice. They should rename both islands.

Record drinking in Cuba

I had a short stopover when back in Iceland and then I continued my summer trip to Canada and Cuba. Canada was business as usual. City tour in Toronto, meeting 2 friends, wet wet wet at the Niagara Falls, wine tasting thingy. Normal. But I had more memories for Cuba. There I got 2 new personal records in drinking. The first one – Cuba Libre: Rum with coke. When I wanted to check in the reception was still closed but the hotel bar was already, or still open shortly before 7 in the morning. To cover some time I had some local drinks. Arriba! Prost! Salute! Visiting a country means also to go with the local flow and taste national food and drinks. Done already. Check! At around 9ish in the morning I had already a quite good drinking load which made the check in more fun, plus the booking of a tour for the next day.

In fact, on the next day I went to an all-inclusive full day holiday resort with food and drinks included.. There I got my second personal best. Since I was drinking through 5 different bars at these resorts, it was no wonder after throwing up first time at around lunch I passed out until 4pm. Earliest knock out for me so far. I lost the rest of the day since my memory wasn't great at all after this hard session.

Open bars in Havana

In general I had the impression there is a bar every 500 meters in Havana, the capital of Cuba. Either a fancy one, a touristic nap such as the Hemingway bar or a one man enterprise! In any case: With a smile and friendliness there was always the option to get free drinks, free accommodation with locals and international people!

In the heat of the Finnish sauna night

Before I flew to my Saudi home I had a short stopover in the Baltics. Latvia and Lithuania for a day each. Just ticking off the countries from my list. Both looked similar to me. Nearly the same as Estonia, which I visited on a previous trip. Full of Russian language and German style buildings, plus a phobia against big brother in the East (Russia). I think all three of these tiny countries could unite to be stronger together. From an outside perspective no one can really point to the differences. The third day in the Baltics was another Finish day, since I wanted to meet my Finnish buddy Vesa. Networking among brothers in arms. He had organized a typical Finnish Sauna session with BBQ, Finnish alcoholic Indulgement and a Sauna place close to the Sea. In total we were four men in the Sauna heat chamber. Everyone had the traditional beer and the aroma of heated wheat reminded me of my childhood: Grilled Toast on BBQ. Same smell! But here we had more fun since the alcohol burnt the heads away at 50 degrees Celsius.

The enlightenment of the Baltic Sea

Normally I don't enjoy having a Sauna session. Had only three or four in my life before. But having it in Finland means travel experience with all the senses. After around 20 minutes I couldn't stand the heat anymore and I tried to ask when we finally can leave this hot place. I didn't know the procedure among the Finnish guys. I believed they can spend hours there. Since they are the founders of sauna culture. I didn't really end my question and promptly my Finnish friend directly answered: "Of course now we can leave". Then he opened the door, started running on the small jetty and jumped off into the cold, unknown water. In the school we had learnt never jump into water that you don't know. Plus I thought the temperature difference might be tremendous. Maybe dying with a heart attack? But when the Fin can do it, I can do it as well since I am ten years younger. So I just followed running and jumping. That was one of my most intense moments in all my travels. In the moment of the dive I felt so clear and sharp. So happy, I could have embraced the whole world. No wonder from

50 Celsius to just 10. My goodness, Life is great. Life is beautiful. The water was hard and sharp and as such I felt like James Bond – Daniel Craig in the movie "Casino Royal" when walking out of the water. World is mine. But where was my bond girl? Nowhere but at least the next Finish beer was at hand. Not bad at all! Kippes!

Waka Waka – This time for Africa again

In October 2013 Africa was calling again. Four countries in one shot and in ten days: Zambia, Zimbabwe, Botswana, Namibia plus South Africa as an airport hub. On the road or better on the plane with me my German friend Christian. He had studied in South Africa and loves to travel. 2 adventurous guys and world tourists on tour. Starting point: Livingstone, to easily and quickly tick off the three neighboring countries. In addition there are the famous Victoria Falls with the stunning devils pool. We planned to have a plunge in it of course. You haven't been in Zambia if you didn't do it. We expected a great experience and even better photographs. The videos on YouTube that we watched before the trip were already amazing.

The hippo in the kid's pool

We expected to book a local travel guy once we checked into our hotel. On our agenda: Cross country taxi rides, swimming in devils pool, maybe some ad-hoc different things. Until our local travel guide arrived we got comfy with a nice bottle of red wine in the little hotel pool. It was just the size of a kid's pool or just a bit bigger than a Jacuzzi. After around half an hour some local Zambian guys including a big fat mama joined us in the pool. It was like in a comedy movie. It felt she had 1000 Kilograms living weight since the water level rose in the now far too small pool. So we took another sip out of the bottle and started some nice African conversations. And again the heat of the sun in combination with the red wine killed all the bad memories. Finally the tourist guide arrived and we booked our trips. Helicopter ride over the water falls, devils pool including breakfast, city and surrounding tour, and finally a water elephant safari in neighboring Botswana. In future I plan to book tours in different countries way in advance, because in some African countries the tourist infrastructure is not as good as in Zambia or South Africa.

Devils pool – The Kick of Zambia

Next day: The devils pool. Finally! We have seen some videos before on the internet and we got really excited. When visiting the Victoria Falls this one is a must. The Victoria Falls are not in close proximity of the Victoria Lake. Even also in Africa but far further up North. The devils pool is a little pot just underneath of the water surface. Up to six people can stand inside. It is about two meters deep. Above it the waves of the Victoria Falls are gliding. Shortly before the edge there is an approx. 80 Centimeters wide flat part which people can lie on. They can even slide and lean over the edge and look directly down in the water. Some brave peeps are only held by their legs by some locals or friends. Otherwise they would crash down into the death. Overall: It looks spectacular when hanging over the edge. Great experience! After the swim and the photo shoot there is a little breakfast nearby with eggs benedict. That makes this trip unforgettable! Nobles!

Crocodile lunch in Zimbabwe

To experience the Victoria Falls fully, you need to cross the border to Zimbabwe. Of cause you can easily get also a new country point by doing it. Synergy effects! With our overpriced driver we went to the border and made the crossing. Already from distance we could hear the tremendous masses of water of the Falls. In rain season it is even more. Then a plunge in the devils pool seems not to be possible. Nevertheless the look was great. We could spot people making photographs on the other side when swimming or standing at or inside the devils pool. Selfie at its best!

Face to Face with Mugabe

After our little sightseeing tour we had dinner in a chic hotel in British colonial style. In the distance we could spot a bridge and the water. I tried for the first time in my life to eat crocodile. It tasted like a mix of chicken and fish. Tres bien! Lecker! In addition we killed one or two bottles of wine while having high philosophic conversations about life, love and peace. My travel friend told me lots of stories about his time in South Africa when he lived and studied there. So he met the president of Zimbabwe in person: Mugabe. He dropped this information just per chance. I asked him how did he meet him and he answered Winni Mandela has introduced both to each other. Then I was stunned. I had never expected that.

Master griller overboard

But also the second African story was worth telling. Christian was once invited to a dinner party on a river boat in Africa. It could have been the river Nile or the Zambesi. It was a descent, chic dressed up party. The BBQ master griller was at the rear deck and grilled sausages, meat and other Indulgement on his BBQ with an open fire. The wind was blowing from the rear. After two to three hours the boat made a 180 degree and returned to the departure place. But then suddenly the wind blew from the front and the master griller caught fire. In his panic he jumped off the boat. He couldn't swim. The river full of crocodiles. The party was over. No help possible for this poor guy.Strangely the crocodile on my plate tasted better in this moment. Maybe I wanted revenge for this BBQ man? But Christian got problems after this story. Either his own story or the pasta he had didn't work well on this day. When we went from Zimbabwe border station through the 200 meters no-man's-land to the station of Zambia he had to puke all the lunch he had before. Over and over again. Luckily his passport was still in good condition to get the necessary stamps.

No injection – no flight

On the next day my friend felt much better. Luckily! Full of our experiences and stories we were looking forward to our departure and ongoing travelling. I headed towards Namibia for two nights while my friend had do go back to Riyadh. Work was calling. But at the Check-In we got surprised and stopped by the lady behind the desk. Every passenger travelling from Zambia to South Africa has to have yellow fever vaccination. At least you need to prove it in a document. No certificate or stamp – no flight. Oh man! We were so thrilled. 90 minutes left to departure. We begged, tried to bribe, and tried our charm. Nothing helped. The check-in lady didn't give pardon. But we were lucky. A taxi driver has only waited for us. He offered a ride to a hospital to get the stamp. The price for the ride was high. Of course. Supply and demand.

Dirty hospital shots

After a hell ride through town we reached a little dark, dirty house. Hospital here we go. My goodness. In my whole life I didn't want to get any treatment there. Only in case of being hit by a car and having lost conciseness. Nothing looked clean in this building. Of course I didn't want to get any injection. We had to pay some extra cash and commit having got a fresh yellow fever shot recently. Quickly the medical lady in charge filled a paper and gave us the yellowish document – proof of injection. Ready. Let's go to the airport. Back to check in and continue flight to South Africa.

Namibia chilling

The next three days I spent relaxed in a lodge west of Windhoek, capital of Namibia. I was the only guest and the host offered fresh made roles in the morning for breakfast, brought the coffee to my little accommodation, and in evening I enjoyed sunset while the wild life had their dinner at the water place nearby. Travel Life is good. Another quick trip successfully concluded.

No Zambia without the devils pool

People who didn't spend any time in devils pool and take a great pic haven't been to Zambia. In addition, people should visit the Hotel Livingstone for a sundowner drink or a dinner. The setting sun in front of the water – a dream. Especially with a nice bottle of Wine, a nice steak or crocodile pieces and nice company. Of course they also have water, halal food and vegan stuff. Never mind. But the sun and the falls remain – in depended from religious belief of sportsman heart. Furthermore I learnt after this trip: Always having 1000 USD at hand or equivalent in local currency. As a backup for a police penalty, ad-hoc bribery or urgent medication.

The Chili ghost of Bhutan

They say Happiness is the states doctrine in Bhutan. It is mentioned in several tourist guide books or you can also find it in different articles. Before arrival I believed it to be more spiritual than Nepal, and more happy smiling people than in Thailand. In addition the photographs from the so called tiger nest, a munch's house high up in the mountains promised very special moments of consciousness – closer to God and endless happiness. Luckily I planned a trip beforehand during my 4 days journey to this place. Of course I planned doing 1 arm pushup videos with the background of this culture highlighted. The landscape of this tiny country was tremendous, a bit like in Switzerland. High trees and mountains. Different artists would have liked to come here to bring these sights to paper. The people are very friendly, having usually a little smile on their faces. But the Thai people smile more – from German perspective, always complaining. They look a bit like Japanese. Additionally, I missed the spirituality and the overwhelming happiness. All marketing gags. Such as the beauty of the Brazilian women. Overrated. Nevertheless I was positively surprised by the kitchen they have. Nearly every dish is made together with spicy chilly. All lovers of hot Indian or Mexican food will fall in love with Bhutan cuisine. Rice, meat, veggie – always hot, spicy with chili! Yummi! The food is on fire!

Running up to the tiger nest

The highlight of this trip is the excursion to the tiger nest. 5 kilometers hiking up a hill. I asked my Tour guide if I could run up and we just meet on the top. Luckily there was only 1 way up. So we wouldn't miss each other or me I wouldn't get lost. Since I was in training for my first marathon in ten years I wanted to do some hill training. As I am not the greatest endurance performer that is still into travelling I tried to use every piece of opportunity to do some exercise. The guide was a bit surprised when I kicked off and left him behind. On top I got a great view above the valley. Unique experience. Light sunshine, 20 degrees Celsius! Perfect light and temperature. I decided to do a headstand with the tiger nest in background. Then followed with a little, fast tour through the building of the munches place. Some photographs and inhaling the spirit, the thin air and some happiness as well.

The fire of the guest family

Then we had to walk down. Next stop: Dinner with a local family. On arrival the family waited for me already with a so called stone bath. After this little hill run it was a bombastic feeling sitting in the heat of the traditional bath. The bath tub was made out of wood. The water was at a descent temperature. At the end of the tube there was a mobile little wall with some holes. Behind this one the hosts put hot, hot, hot stones. These came directly out of an open fire that was burning outside the house. The heat of the stones warmed the water. Since I was a bit tired but still having enough energy to read I enjoyed having a bath for around one hour. My Tour guide took his bath right next to me but after nearly ten minutes he got bored, or it was too hot for him. The following dinner was like this: Chili with rice and meat. The kids of the house sang in the local language some songs for my entertainment. This reminded me of my home stay in a village in Kirgizstan where I also got a mini concert. Again, I thought for little money exploring strange, new worlds can be so easy and satisfying. The German writer Goethe once said a line a like that: "Here I am. Here I am human. Here I can enjoy life". or similar, he mentioned it in one of his writings. While a lot of other friends and colleagues I know usually spend their vacation in five star hotels I believed travelling in this way brings me at least a deeper approach to the countries and places I visit. Finally I found the happiness the people talk about when speaking about Bhutan!

1 Jumping into the icy water of the Antarctic

2 Swimming in the devils pool in Zambia

3 Hand shake with the 20 Dollar Putin in Moscow

4 Together with friends in Hamam in Istanbul

5 An animal friend on the island of Madagascar

6 Mud package on the island of St. Lucia in the Caribbean

7 Over the top in the Skybar of Panama City

8 Night over in a kettle farm in Kirgizstan

9 Trying the local Sport in Seychelles

10 Show fight in Jordan

11 Relaxation at a wedding safari in South Africa

12 Hot bath in the Blue Lagoon in Iceland

13 Triathlon training in Ghana

14 Upside down in the height of Bhutan

15 Judo training with kids in Africa

16 Embracing the World after river safari in Burundi

17 Happy hand stand on the Cook Islands

18 Judo training in Kirgizstan

19 Ironman Finisher in Klagenfurt, Austria

20 Visit a living volcano in Vanuatu

21 Together with a tour guide in Senegal

22 Dressing like the locals in Georgia

23 Animal life at a water safari in Botswana

24 Christian helps handicapped Kids in Kathmandu

25 Finisher Smile with Triathlon friend Jo on Mauritius

26 Plan to visit Christian and his family in Brazil in 2019

27 Rocky beach on Nauru island

28 All eyes to the right in Peru

29 View from the only hotel of the stilt village in Benin

30 Staying in this cube in Mexico

31 Wedding crasher in Minsk

32 Swimming in the cold waters of Antarctic

33 Sunset in Bermuda Island

34 Natural pool in the Caribbean

35 Teaching a young boy hand stand in middle of Africa

36 Happy jump after 50 Km Dead Sea Marathon in Jordan

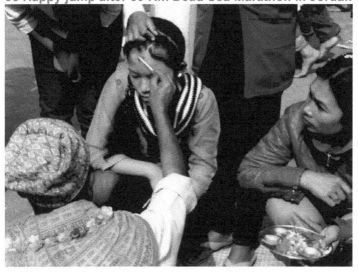

37 Traditional facial paint in Nepal

38 Sightseeing tour in Uruguay

39 Stunning landscape in Greenland

40 World War II bunker at Omaha Beach in the Normandy

41 British-Pakistani friend encouraged me to go to Karachi

42 Travel partners in crime n beauty: Paul and Stephanie

43 Quick shot from Marshall Islands

44 Having a traditional hot stone bath in Bhutan

45 Handstand at the overnight camping in the Antarctic

46 Some souvenirs from Senegal at beach hotel in Dakar

47 First steps in Tango in Buenos Aires

48 In Paradise of Mauritius you cannot take a bad picture

49 Florent from France offers tours in Saudi Arabia

50 Entertaining kids in Kiribati

51 Saudi Biker friend Monther exploring the world

2014 – Race hard. Party hard!

On the Road again – this time the Balkans

Road trip on the Balkans together with another American friend. We had already done Serbia (Belgrade where I did another Marathon in this year) and Macedonia and were currently in Romania. Suddenly my friend wanted to go to Moldova. That would be really close. In fact he was right but I didn't plan it before and the calculation wasn't that great for it since I planned riding everyday around five hours with the car and having enough time for sightseeing and party. But now he got also infected by collecting countries and finally we agreed on adjusting the travel plan to tick off Moldova as well. Nevertheless, with our rental car we were not allowed to pass the border from Romania to Moldova. Taxi only. Walking also possible but not that great.

Hitchhikers Guide through Galati

Therefore we quickly stopped a taxi at the border town of Galati / Galatz to get the Moldavian country point. The taxi driver agreed to transport us through the border checkpoint just shortly after the border and then quickly return. Maybe just stopping for a toilet stop and a coffee. Country point is country point. We were already late and made this extra time just for the stamp in the passport. We drove around 30, 40 minutes through Galati to the border. Only then the driver recognized that he neither had his passport with him nor a permission to cross the border. Well, back to the roots. Another taxi driver. Another ride. The next one I directly asked if he had all necessary documents with him. I even let him to show the documents. So I had proper proof. Remembering my army days, sometimes you have to play stupid when you want to control people. I did not want to waste my time again going to border and again to return. Crossing the border was quite successful. Easy peasy. 10 minutes coffee break and then return. We still had a 5 hours' drive before us and to cover half of Romania from the east to the west to Bucharest.

Delay, delay, delay

But the fast track through the border was closed. We had to line up. Three lines of cars waited already for hours. It went very slowly. The check of cars and people took ages. After two hours a group of motorbikes passed by. They could easily cross the border. I already thought to go with him by paying them 20 dollars, or, but in fact we didn't know exactly where we had parked our car on the other side. Only the taxi driver knew. Stupid us! Since my impatience came into the game I went directly to the border police officer and tried my luck. When he recognized that we are American and German he directly said we could come forward and easily pass. Hallelujah. The rest of the other people came from the former Eastern bloc and I guess they were properly checked since smuggling at this border crossing point seemed to a good business. But we were just easy tourist on the hunt for another country point.

Pacific Island hopping

In this summer I went to the Pacific. Samoa, Vanuatu, Tonga, and Fiji. Quickly I passed the first three islands with each one or two days. The highlights were in Vanuatu, the visit to a living volcano, and the tip here is to stay overnight in a tree house. In Samoa the cutest thing I have seen so far were the little piglets running on the streets hunting for food. Tonga – a good spot to swim with humpback whales. Usually I don't really like diving or snorkeling but I guess this opportunity doesn't come every day. But bad luck! it was stormy and rainy on the day I had booked the trip. However I stayed inside my little palm cottage and thought: "Country point is country point. Tonga – Check!"

Go for Fiji Fun

Even having all planned country points I was a bit disappointed about missing the sightseeing activities due to the bad weather conditions. Finally, I reached Fiji for two days and I hoped to have some fun. Already on arrival in the airport I quickly recognized that these islands are best for tourism. While I was walking through immigration I started checking out the prospects. So many full day and half day tour options. A big selection of diving, snorkeling, dinner cruises, fun boat trips and and and. After getting the Fiji stamp the next two days were planned already. Check! Now quickly to the hotel and complete payment for the trips. Fiji here we come.

From golden beers to golden girls

For budget oriented travels but also for middle class peeps the "Smugglers Cove" is a good choice.

Private beach, small pool, bars, and a cool atmosphere makes the stay a dream. Great sunsets are guaranteed since the hotel is facing towards west. Best you enjoy the sunset with both of the local beer brands: Fiji Bitter or Fiji Gold. After my island trips filled with snorkeling, sun bathing, swimming, and meeting new peeps from all over the world at night. Another Fiji Gold, or off to bed and get ready for the next flights. Saving energy and calories. All tables in the open garden were taken. Couples here. Party groups there. Talking bullshit to peeps to get company at a table? Bullshit! Best is for other people to start talking to you. But with average size and look it was quite difficult. Also no one from the day trip was present. Best is sharing a big table with 2 blondes. Playing the innocent. That is always working. The horse of troy is calling. Then ordering strange food, crazy drink, smiling and eye contact. Easy peasy talk is saved! Good luck! 2 other blonde roommates joined later on and the final night in Fiji ended with four Fiji Golden girls.

Running three countries in 210 minutes

After the summer another Balkan trip ahead. This time, starting off with running a marathon at the beginning of the trip. Since nearly one year I increased my running skills by training more and more in Riyadh plus reading funny books from the German hobby athlete Achim Achilles. Slowly I developed the idea to run a marathon in at least half of the countries I visit. But ticking off countries would still be my number 1 priority. In September I aimed for my fastest marathon. As an average endurance person I thought 3.30 hours could be a good one. Once an old friend said: "Hey dude, marathon running starts only with sub 3.30". I never believed I could make it. But I tried to apply tips from co-runners, diet tips (less drinks, more fruits and lean meat). So I registered for a 3-Countries marathon in South Germany at the Bodensee. Start in the German town of Lindau. In between, Switzerland. Finish in Austrian town of Bregenz. Of course I planned a quick visit in Liechtenstein to get this country ticked off.

Carbo load at Octoberfest: Prost!

Arrival in Munich just before the marathon and there was the Octoberfest going on. A good chance to meet old and new friends. Just before a marathon where I wanted to get a best time – not a good idea. But also at the biggest beer festival of the world you can do carbo loading and drink alcohol free beer or apple juice. Both are looking similar to the normal beer and are also served in the big Maas stones. My party friends didn't really recognize any difference. Otherwise I would have to tell them why I am not drinking etc. bla bla. Nevertheless two hours of celebrating with them is enough since the logic and intelligence of intoxicated peeps is falling dramatically. Reason enough to head off to the marathon destination.

5 minutes Coffee break without a coffee in Liechtenstein

My hotel was in Bregenz the Austrian town where the Marathon finished. Since there was a bit time before checking in I got a taxi and told the driver: "Hey let us go to Liechtenstein. There we will drink a coffee and head directly back." For 100 Euro and a coffee for the driver I could get easily the country Liechtenstein. Cheap. Cheap. No bad deal. The driver thought in the first place that I am a rich guy that just wanted to bring some cash to the tiny country and save it from the tax hunters in Germany. But he was wrong. However on that day no café was opened for us. So had a just a 5 minutes talk in a little town just behind the border (thanks to Schengen) no border security in place anymore: Having a deep breath and then back to Austria. Liechtenstein: Check! Mission accomplished!

Race plan readiness

After registering for the marathon I visited the open lake side opera spot in Bregenz. The view of the lake in the background of the opera stage was stunning. Performances must be tremendous. However having these dreams in my mind, focus on the race. I knew a colleague wanted to meet me after for a dinner. I asked him to wait at the 30 Kilometers marker with a can of Red bull to boost my strength for the last 10 Kilometers, to give me the wings I might need at that point of time. I was curious if he would make it.

Personal best but Red Bull flew too late

Then: Race day. 18 degrees, light sunshine, Perfect running conditions. I placed myself behind the pacemaker of a 3.30 finishing time and could hold the pace. The lake was nearly the whole time on the right side but I didn't have really the landscape in my mind since I listened to my body, felt it, and checked when to drink and to eat. I had a good run, sticked to the pacemaker and at the end just at kilometer 40 I heard someone shouting: "Bracki, Bracki here is your Red Bull". Ha! that was my colleague. That made me smile and pushed me more since it was a tight game to stay under 3.30. I could only shout back that we would meet in the finish area. I didn't want to lose pace to get the drinks he brought for me. Yes! I did 3.28. Happy with the medal and the waiting colleague! Super! He picked me up with his Porsche. Nobles. Great! I invited him to a big Schnitzel and Beer high in a mountain restaurant with a great view over the landscape. A great day!

Balkan country tick offs

The race was just the kick start for the next days on the Balkans where I ticked off Montenegro with the stunning old towns of Kotor. Slovenia, with its capital Ljubljana and again Albania with surprisingly lots of bunkers and castles spread in landscape of the mountains. Since I became now more and more a runner and triathlete somehow I wanted to combine travelling with these sports activities. Racing at the beginning of the trips, and to get rewarded afterwards with drinks and food. Swim, bike, run, drink, and repeat.

First Saudi race then Bahraini party

The last 3 countries marathon showed that I had become a descent runner. I slowly started with swimming and cycling in the months before. But during my first bike out in spring time I broke my elbow. 3 months down time, with no sports over the summer. At least I could travel. Since I had good physio and orthopedic treatment I could recover quickly. But I was still not yet a triathlete since I didn't finish yet a triathlon of any distance. After personal best in the 3- countries Marathon I was highly motivated but in Riyadh the season was nearly over and there was no triathlon scheduled anymore. My first one should be in the east of the country in Ras Tanourah. Olympic Distance (1500 meters swim in the Arabic Gulf, 40 Kilometers cycling and 10 Kilometers of running). Due to proper planning I could arrange a Work-Sport-Party weekend out of it. Thursday business meeting in Dammam close to Ras Tanourah), Friday: Race and directly after crossing the border to neighboring Bahrain to have a reward of partying. Racing and partying. All planned with my French Triathlon friend Sylvain.

Water of survival

Race day: I was only afraid of the swim, as it was my first time ever in open water. Normally swim training takes place in a 25 meters swimming pool in Riyadh. I learnt freestyle just half a year ago. Excitement was on! Pushing myself to the next level and fighting against the water. Cycling would be ok. I only needed to avoid falling down. The run will be easy I believed. Out of all three sports that's my strength. Yallah here we go. The first shock after 200 meters! There are waves in the water, and no line on the bottom. OMG! "Will I die today?", I asked myself after swallowing a lot of salty water. The pool swim was so easy; even though I didn't like it, the water was flat like a table. And here there was another wave, Fuck! Where are the safety boats? What shall I do? I tried it with breast strokes: Better orientation and less water into my mouth. I could outbalance the waves and breathe nearly normally. At the beginning, all new things in life are not easy. The swim had the so called Australian exit: After 750 meters out to the land, circling a flag pole and back in. I was so shocked that I stood still and considered just doing the half distance today. It would be also a triathlon but just the sprint distance. After nearly two minutes maybe I thought: "Today I don't want to die – but I have to go back in. If I want to continue with this sport I need to." If you go to hell then do it in style! I sprinted into the water and started swimming with a mixture of breast stroke and freestyle.

Against the wall of Saudi heat

Finally out of the water, my time was in accordance to my standards. I felt ok. Next, the bike! Since I was one of the last guys out of the water I could easily catch up and I passed people in front of me. That was a great motivation. In addition I trusted my strength on the run at the end. No crash. Great! Now only running, get a finisher medal and t-shirt, pack up and then off to Bahrain to celebrate. But already after 2 kilometers I hit the wall. No energy. Weak. Totally exhausted. The 35 degrees heat, the sun, the humidity – all seem to kill me on this run. The air burned in my lungs. I had to walk even. I felt so terrible. But my French race buddy had the same issues. Since he was more experienced and better skilled, he had small lead. At the end we were both done, but happy to have finished the distance. My first triathlon! Super. But now it was time to power up, bikes and gear into the car and head to Bahrain.

Indian struggle in Bahrain

We had to quickly go to Bahrain. Other expats and Saudi's had the same thought, like every weekend and the roads were busy. The time was tight because we needed to find our hotel, check in, shower, and off via Taxi to Radisson Blu hotel for champagne brunch. There we aimed for the 50 US Dollar Champagne brunch. I already knew how awesome this drinking and eating event was. Only later I thought we should have stayed directly at Radisson Blu to save some time but now it was too late. But if you don't expect problems there will always be coming some. At the reception desk of the hotel the Indian service guy didn't want to let us check in our expensive bicycles. The 4 people suite that we booked would be too small. I tried the African bribery way with 20 US Dollars. No chance. Then I got more excited and a bit angry. I don't want to miss my brunch just because one guy that doesn't have a clue about the values of the bikes (that we didn't want to leave behind in the car). I said at the end that in India 4 Billion people live on

20 Square meters and now here in Bahrain in our 4 people suite we cannot fit in 2 extra bikes? Cannot believe it! Ok. The comparison was not the best, it was a bit exaggerated, racist and not fair but sometimes such argumentation lines help. Apparently my bullshit talk didn't help. Now I pulled out the biggest killer: "Where is the manager?" Finally she arrived and we could convince her – I believe it was my friend who used his French-mon-amour-Cherie-charm to let us check in. Then: Hotel room, Shower, Dress up. Of course I we ordered a taxi at reception before going to shower. I think this time the German planning came into play. Now: Ready, steady, drink!

Quick into the head makes you mad

As we had arranged beforehand two of our expat friends were already waiting for us at the restaurant. They had a lead of several glasses and plates and were already in a good mood. Even without their level of alcohol, they were happy to see us. Having fun with friends, is always better than just partying alone. In any case, I planned to rapidly catch up with both of them. That seemed no problem since my French triathlon buddy and me were still a bit dehydrated, didn't eat at all after the race and as a sports person you get "head kicked" much easier. Despite these facts, I tried the both handed drinking style. Right and left hand with champagne. Ex and hopp – rein in den Kopp – as we Germans say. Prost! In combination with some cold beer, great food our lamps went off quite quickly. For an after party we were not ready anymore and slept straight through from 9 until 7 in the morning. Bam! Alcohol in the blood but happy with the Triathlon finisher medal!

Reward drinking after races

Even loving eating and drinking I tried to apply special diets without having alcohol and meat. I believed I had to compensate a lack of yearlong endurance training, experience and talent. Even after reading books and tips from other sports people having a more veggie diet would be healthy and productive for triathlon sport. Side effect: Looking lean, hot and being fast! Bam! Bam! Bam! 1 Kilogram less means 1 percent speed increase. I read that somewhere. But to totally give up any kind of meat or drinks I couldn't do. So I start having reward eating and drinking after races. If I want to drink more and party more I needed to do more races and training. Easy! At the end it would be an average and moderation of training and nutrition. All balanced out on the long term.

Next level: Dubai International Triathlon

After struggling in Ras Tanourah on the Saudi East Coast I signed up for a Half Ironman Man Triathlon Distance in neighboring United Arab Emirates. In the Emirate of Dubai there I had to swim 1.9 Km, cycle 90km and run a half marathon of 21 km. Together with a Pilipino colleague we planned driving 12 hours by car from Riyadh to Dubai. The companion would be a verbal punching bag for me. Since I didn't want to ride all the way alone I needed someone to talk to plus in case of emergency I wouldn't be alone. Hey passing Saudi streets and deserts it's not the safest idea. Flying could have been an option. But I didn't want to transport my bike yet since in this stage my technical bike set up skills were as poor as my orientation skills.

Bike porn in transition zone

After a short stopover in a random 1 star hotel at the border we headed towards Dubai passing camels, sand dunes, and more sand, followed by the skyscrapers of Abu Dhabi, and its picturesque buildings full of glass and metal. On arrival in the race registration I was overwhelmed by the nice and fancy expensive bikes. There is a reason why people speak about bike porn at such races. People invest up to 10.000 Dollars to pimp their ride. Carbon, ultra-light, super gears, disc wheels, and, and, and.

Triathlon sport against midlife crisis?

Every one shows what they got and what they want to spend for this sport. It looks like that this triathlon sport is made for middle aged guys in the midlife crisis somehow. If you are in your 30ies or 40iest you have reached already a status in business, family life and you seek for new adventures and challenges. Plus you got the money to spend on it. Your life is in order somehow. You made your career already or gave up on doing it. People are married with kids, divorced, still single or whatever. You know already how to plan trainings and when to pull it out. When you have the passion for this sport you create time easily. If you are dedicated / committed there are no excuses. There are no bad weather conditions, no family or job is coming in your way. You just manage everything around your sport. Once I read the statement that Ironman Triathlon World champs are the most egoistic people on earth. In moderation this is also true for all the amateurs and age groupers but on a different scale.

Race hard, party harder

The race went for me like planned. Since I improved a bit on my swimming and knowing what was ahead. My swim part went well. Ok. The swim leg happened in a bay. Flat water no waves. But swimming for me is always a challenge. So I was happy to be out of the water. For the bike, I hold my horses to have enough power left for the running part. Even my Triathlon friend Wolle told me before I could smash the bike part since I am a strong runner. But I was too much afraid to have such a disaster like before. But I underestimated the sun. Burning like hell on the run part. Nevertheless I flew past nearly all the people in front of me. Great feeling. Terrific! With tears in my eyes I finished my first half Ironman. After some anxiety before the race, total relief now. Of course I could have gone faster, but that's a typical sentence of a triathlete. But anyways! Now focus on the reward: food and drinks. Another champagne brunch in a Skybar of Dubai. Great view. Great experience. Nap time. Massage, and then for a dinner meeting with a friend from my study times. She had organized dancing and partying with some of her lady friends in the Music hall, a local dance theater. 1 man and 6 ladies. Best reward ceremony! Great. Dancing until 4 in the morning. Then back to the hotel, sleeping 4-5 hours, breakfast with another Dubai couple and then heading straight back home to Riyadh for a 12 hours ride. Stupid idea. Every hour 1 Red Bull or a coffee. It was not fun and this ride was more exhausting than the half ironman including dancing party after. Never again! However I survived the triathlon and the Saudi roads and was happily home!

Seven countries in one blow on a cruise

In all my life I was wondering how a cruise would be. All my ex-ladies, wives or whatever, it meant that we were too young for it. Every time, I made the comprise, but this time I planned this trip alone even booking a double room to save some money and believing some of my friends would join this incredible experience. I checked different cruise lines and routes but found the German boat liner

AIDA cruise has the best offer concerning time, money and new country points for me. Flying to different island countries, such as St. Lucia, Grenada, Barbados, St. Vincent and the Grenadines, and others would be too expensive and is not that practical. In addition, I fell in love with this driving hotel with pools, gym, spa, night clubs, and restaurants and so on. And the best: Nearly every day in the morning waking up in a new country. The dream.

The last call girl – French! What else?

Shortly before the departure a French lady friend gave her agreement to join the ride. Only condition: Separated beds since her boyfriend wouldn't find it nice. However, I believed if my GF would go on a Caribbean cruise with another man I would really not consider this kind of relationship. Anyways, I was happy to have some nice company, shared costs, and always nice photographs from me since I believed a woman as travel companion is always on photograph hunting mode. Even I had fun collecting new countries it was a great experience to see the difference in landscape and vegetation of these places. There were national parks, dream beaches, volcanic islands and rain forests. All in the mix of the Caribbean. But the guests had a free choice. They could have also stayed onboard. But hey: if you land in a dream island why not discover it?

Loosing nerves and travel book

Despite all different impressions one shock moment I will never forget. On the island of Grenada I lost my little travel book the so called "Globetrotters Logbook". Even I had bought it only for 10 Euro in the meantime it got up in the value to 300 bucks for me since I filled it up with little postal or immigration stamps per country I visited so far. The flight tracker was already filled up since only 100 flights were possible to fill in. I had so many personal messages in this book, extra little souvenirs like addresses from hotels, restaurants or little stickers from all over the planet.

Seek and you shall find

I lost it in a national park. Oh my god. I believed I needed to buy a new one and start all over again with ordering postal stamps to mark the countries I visited already. Sounds stupid, but once you have reached more than 150 countries you would pay a fortune to get it back. Also, all the personal memories are gone. Only the old memories in the head would remain. It was clear that I was moody all day. I was so disappointed and sad. I didn't know what to do. At around 6pm in the evening two ladies knocked at my door and showed me my book. There must be a lovely god in heaven. I offered them all drinks on me for the whole night – so happy I was. They had found the book lying in the grass. They both also did the day trip to the same national park. Luckily I had already a little sticker from the AIDA cruise in the book with cabin number. And also luckily they were both on the same boat as guests. Lucky man I am!

2015 – Ironman Beach Body Show

South African wedding

Shortly after this amazing Caribbean cruise I headed off again to South Africa because I was invited for the wedding of my German-South African Travel buddy Christian. After the wedding and spending New Year's Eve in Cape Town and ticking off the country of Malawi further up North. However, the wedding should be great since my friend planned 3 days bachelor party. BBQ plus Safari on day 1 – men only babies. Day 2 was focused on people from abroad in German-Bavarian-Octoberfest style (everyone dressed up in Dirndl or Lederhosen) and day 3, finally the wedding celebration. NYE at the waterfront in Cape town. Hallejullah!

Endurance training in Malawi

After all the partying in South Africa I was off to Malawi where I stayed for four long days. While I could order easily day tours on arrival at previous trips to see and experience the country I couldn't do it this time. I stayed in a middle class hotel. Calling a travel agent? No way! Sim cards – No! Landline phone – No! This hotel was a big disappointment. I didn't even ask for Wi-Fi. Somehow I could manage to get some day trips for outrages prices. I could visit some boring paintings in caves or little national parks. In addition, I went to Lake Malawi. But a friend warned me not to bathe in it, since it is full of bacteria. Therefore no bathing fun at all. The only thing I tried to do was running through all the black people in downtown and having at least some mileage for my endurance training. With a bright red colored shirt and white face I was the strangest thing then I believed. I didn't feel safe at all since I was a light spot in-between the poor looking crowd. If a white man comes to Africa he must have money. It's not racist it's a matter of fact. Therefore I changed every day my route, ran zigzag and made sure to be at the hotel before darkness. Safety first.

Malta – Italy- Arabesque Flair

Some weeks later I was off to Malta. There I signed up for the local marathon. I aimed for a new personal best time since it is a slightly downhill course, every 5 km equipped with a music band

and stunning scenery. I became more and more aware that I can combine ticking off countries and run marathons or do triathlons worldwide. So I could embrace all the spirit of the countries in a much better way, meeting new local and international people for exchanging travel and race experiences and widen my horizon. Great. Travelling could be more intensive this way. Either it's swimming against the current, riding a bike up a hill or running on a sandy beach – there is always a country related challenge. And I wanted to experience them. Easiest way is to join a marathon run. For a triathlon you have to bring your own bike or you have to rent it. This time it should be the islands of Malta. Italian style with Arabic background. Would be an interesting mix! Unluckily I got an injury before so I could only do some walking through the great capital Valetta. I felt like I was in Italy with all the nice buildings, columns, Italian like dishes and drinks.

Abu Dhabi Du

For summer 2015 I scheduled my first Ironman Triathlon race. Nearly all my social life and travelling was dominated by this upcoming challenge. After my little injury I had to catch up and do a race in another beautiful environment: Abu Dhabi at the beginning of March. I knew this place from previous trips with Formula 1 race track, great bars and restaurants, nice beaches and mosques. It's just a great place for sightseeing, having a short break, and a doing a short triathlon. This time it was again an Olympic Distance (1.5 Km Swim, 40 km on the bike and 10 km run). I really hoped my cranky leg would hold up against all the punishments. Together with Triathlon friend Clemens we headed to the east of Saudi Arabia transporting our bicycles in a jeep. Hotel Check-in, Race registration, pre-race pizza, pasta party, and race...felt like a routine already. Descent time at the finish line. Bam. Bam. Bam. Now the after party with reward drinking could start. Per chance I met a another triathlon girl that I tried to conquer by chasing away another friend by saying: "Hey you got your girl at home. This one is mine" in fact that was the greatest take away from this trip: Having now a travel – triathlon companion with some benefits.

Honey moon without a wedding

Together with my new triathlon friend there were common training sessions. Even though not that ambitious for an Ironman she was still engaged in swimming, biking and running. To have some synergetic training and travelling opportunity we went to the Seychelles to enjoy life. Since my impatience came into play she had one condition: " I only travel with you when you don't propose". Easy peasy. I just want to have training and fun in the sun. I was rather concerned about my harsh training regime and nutrition plan. Usually people get out of shape once they are dating. I strongly believed that too much drinks and Indulgement would harm my ironman preparation. Or, just living from love and air? Never mind!, we might handle that in a proper way and any physical activity would burn calories. The Seychelles were not only great because of the red hot chili pepper girl, the islands offered lots of beaches for relaxing, running, swimming and sun bathing. Open water swims were a dream. On the small island of Prasline cars are forbidden so it was easy to use your bicycles to pull out some mileage. In addition, there was the local annual carnival. Pure entertainment. Lots of colors! Great!

Ironman travel party weeks

Finally it was there. Summer time, 2 Ironman Triathlons coming up within 3 weeks, and a wedding to attend in Germany. In addition, some new countries to visit of course, Slovakia, and all Latin American countries between Mexico and Panama. Average stayover – 1.5 days. Travelling by bus, plane, boat, and car. Bam! Bam! Bam! Ready to rumble. Kick off in Klagenfurt, Austria. Of course I could have trained more for the triathlons and be better prepped, but that's always the case. A typical excuse for a triathlete, but now focuses! Training done, tapering as well, carbo-loading finished. Now getting ready and all the positive vibes that the super landscape can offer. In the army there were phrases such as: "Learn suffering without complaints or don't complain just fight." So I tried to push it all the way. Even in the water when having cramps I wanted to push it. Yeah. Again I was happy out of the water, onto the bike, and finally the run. Overwhelmed by the atmosphere of the cheering crowd. Great! Breathtaking scenery around the race.

Schnitzel protein reload in Vienna

The next day spending with Austrian friends in Vienna and schnitzel killing plus a quick boat ride down the Danube river to Bratislava. Slovakia as country to be ticked off. In addition with a big plater of all different kinds of protein rich meat. Check! Return to Vienna taking off to Berlin to Hotel Mama. Birthday Champagne Breakfast on 2nd July and celebrating Ironman finish.

Birthday – Wedding travelling in East Germany

Then via train to Dresden. Evening close to Semper opera birthday dinner on me. 20 people including me happy like hell. Porkshenks, Radeberger Beer and summer feeling. Great. Next morning in a castle wedding German – Lebanese Wedding celebration of Stephanie and Paul. One of my besties. Of course: Being in charge of a nice wedding speech for this great couple. They love each other and love to marry each other. So they repeated the ceremony later on Lebanon plus a Christian style on in Frauenkirche in Dresden. So they got famous, being show model for the Frauenkirche wedding magazine. Even got coverage on Middle eastern TV for their binational love and travel affairs.

Another great week of planning and conduction done. Check! Party not too hard since only 2 weeks left to Ironman in Zurich. Had booked another big race. Hopefully the body will not be on strike and will be fully recovered. Challenge accepted. My motivation: The new finisher medal ahead and wanted to win a bet against my French triathlon friend that offered Ritz Carlton brunch in case of the finish of 2 Ironmans in 3 weeks' time. Peng!

Mexico to Panama in 2 weeks

Pain. Pain. Pain. Not yet recovered, I could finish Zurich 90 minutes slower than the first one. But hey! done it. Waiting for the Ritz Carlton brunch, but before that, I was off to Latin America to check out some nice countries on my list. Cancun here I come. Hotel was a bit aside of the American hotel castles and directly at a local restaurant. No need for the menu I called just: "Burrito and Tequila Muchacho" No party time and ready for celebration. March, march, another Tequila! From starting point in Cancun with my ironman body ready for the beaches in Mexico, a bit sightseeing, dancing, more tequila. Off to Belize, the snorkeling and diving paradise. Snorkeling with sharks. Flight hopping through Guatemala, Honduras, Nicaragua and ending in Panama. While other back packers need 2-3 months for this trip just 2 weeks would be enough for me. Limited vacation time and a country point is a country point. Focus on the highlights of each place. Sometimes it worked, sometimes not. Never mind. Mentally I was already planning the next tours.

Hills of Whiskey on Mauritius

Already at the beginning of my triathlon ambitions my French race buddy Sylvain gave me the hint to go for a triathlon on the picturesque island of Mauritius. Every year in November there is the Indian Ocean triathlon. Great landscape, swimming in clear water with the fishes, super family like ambience – and another new country point. Perfect. To have a good cost-benefit ratio I planned the combination with Madagascar. The flight is very expensive though. But in the mix with the island of lemurs, it would be more practical. Due to the fact of staying only 3,5 days in this paradise I had to convince my Scottish Triathlon partner to travel with me. Usually I figured out that country collectors and rapid travelers leave their wifes alone or travel though life as a single since the partner is usually the weakest link by moaning, wasting time for selfies, and money (better quality accommodation and dining out) etc. etc. But I strongly believe if people don't travel with me they will never go to these strange new worlds. However no one ever complained about the travel packages that I wrapped up. Or they are all just smart and polite?

In Mauritius there is the whiskey label called "Chamarel". Different sub brands exist. There is a steep hill with the same name. As a triathlete you have the chance to climb it in the race first and after you can have a nice glass full of this yummy drink. Disadvantage for the local race is the strong current, the ugly beauty of the water. At the end the beach run of 12 kilometers there was a little compensation payback for the tough water swim part at the beginning. At least there was the whiskey Indulgement for after party.

Wake up calls by lemurs on Madagascar

Since I have been doing this triathlon endurance sport, first comes the hard painful work, followed by Indulgement of the beach life, adventures and reward partying. That makes the good balance of sports and party life. After three days in Mauritius I was off to Madagascar with a nice bottle of "Chamarel" in my hand luggage. A mix of adventure in the bush and at the beach was waiting. 3 days only. I had limited vacation time, like always. Expensive flights though. The highlight of the island is in the North. Diver's paradise Nosy Bee, Miss Scotland wanted to see that point but we didn't have time of course. Go east was the direction to follow. The road conditions were awful. Typically Africa. Therefore we made a booking with a local travel agency offering us a mixture of summer sun, beach, and rumble in the jungle. Bamboos cottage after a long pick up ride from the airport in the capital was an obligation. Short sleep, due to hell of noise in the morning. A long high tone made us stand up in bed. Beside lots of mosquitoes and other little living things the noise was the killer in parallel to the humid heat. Finally we figured the noise was coming from these monkey like animals – the lemurs. These little bastards were very naughty but sweet. The trial to smuggle them home failed of course. In a little park they were climbing on us and jumping there and back. Four, five of these ones were on top of us. Soft and cozy with big ears. Yeah!

Beach massages with live cooking

Via Jeep we went further East, off to our beach bungalow. Overall the meals on Madagascar were really awful. Having eaten worldwide I could say the food so far in this place: Bad, bad, bad! Positive: Bungalow only 10 meters away from the beach. Soft sand and easy water. With camera and extra water in hand a 5 kilometers beach run ended in a half marathon. The sand was great, the beach flat, and whenever necessary running off into the waves. Swim-Run selfies followed. A great triathlon vacation so far. After training comes the massage with beach view and looking at young boys playing soccer in the sand. That's vacation. Of course having drinks all the way. But the best came in the evening by having a fresh fish, lobster locally cooked on a BBQ and perfectly served. Great. Travel life is great!

Overrated Mauritius but sweet lemurs

To sum this trip up: Mauritius is overrated. The beaches are ok. Seychelles, Maldives, Thailand, Dubai are better concerning paradise and recreation feeling. But the "Chamarel Whiskey" is the nonplus ultra. Same counts for the sweet lemurs in Madagascar, the highlight of this trip.

Home sweet home for Xmas

As mentioned before sometimes a world traveler has to go home for checking up on the family, telling travel stories, celebrating Xmas and of course combining the home flights with new countries. After five years in the sandpit, for Xmas I planned to go this time home for the lovely people on the home front. The red flame had to join this great trip with average staying of 2 days in each place. On the tight agenda there were cities in Germany followed by Barcelona, Andorra, and Morocco. Barcelona – Casablanca 80 Euros return. Idiotic if you don't make this deal. Schedule like that: Riyadh – Germany (Berlin, Potsdam, Dresden, Jueterbog) – Spain (Barcelona) – Morocco (Casablanca, El Jadidah) – Barcelona – Andorra – Barcelona – UK (London). Ten days would be enough for all this travelling. With will power, German planning, proper energy and money management – easy peasy. Ah yes: A New Year's Eve 10 Kilometers run inclusive NYE party in Barcelona add on.

German speed a la ICE train

Thanks to German Bahn speed train and punctuality including rental car 4 German cities could be covered rapidly to visit family and friends, and in total 6 or 7 different Xmas markets. It felt like having 50 Gluhwein, Xmas snacks and other Indulgement all the way. Even for hard core travelers on day 4 we had to put into the game a relaxing day. 5 star Pullmann hotel in Barcelona with a roof top heated pool and champagne on xmas day. That's the plan. But the weak point is always the other half, and in this case it was the hotel. No pool, no roof top, but it did have champagne. Hot tub in hotel room didn't even function. At least an upgrade and a voucher! Ok. Fair enough. Enjoying the ambience of the Catalan capital with some friends. Drinking Spanish wine with nice company – always great.

Ski and shopping stopover Andorra

From Barcelona it is only a stone throw, or better a bus tour, to Andorra. A tiny country in-between France and Spain. Country point 2 hours away. 1 night check. People come here for skiing, drinking and shopping, or for country point collection. Nevertheless, we had a mix of everything. Riding on a snowmobile, dining in, drinking outside, and stunning selfies in the snow for the social media community. In addition, warming up in the city's thermal bath. Back to Barcelona the next day. Another night in this nice city followed by 2 nights stopover on the west coast of Morocco. Arrival in Casablanca and taxi march to El Jadidah. 5 star resort was waiting with buggy rides, Xmas food, massage treatment and beach runs. Country point included. Check! Last night of the year in Barcelona celebrating in a night club in the underground. Short sleep and off to airport for visiting family and friends in London for a night including a quick four hours sightseeing run-walk passing Big Ben, the flyer, Thames River and all the other sights people know. The old year ended as 2016 will be: Fast travelling, sport and party – all in da mix.

2016 – Antarctica calling

Travelling to the best time

In this year I wanted to have a new personal best time in another Ironman triathlon race: Ironman Frankfurt beginning of July. The first half year I completed different fast races in the Middle East. The times were promising. Another milestone should be the half Ironman Triathlon in Busselton, west coast of Australia. Around 5 hours finish – not that bad for me. Could have been faster of course especially when I consider I was riding on a rented road bike.

Quick into Karachi and quick out

However, travel wise I combined this trip with the country of Pakistan. Just for one night in Karachi since I was a bit afraid of the security situation. "Pakistan? Is it not too dangerous there?" my friends asked when I revealed my travel plans. In fact I believed to get killed either by a suicide bomber or by an American drone. Therefore I only wanted to go for just 1 night to Karachi. Quick in, quick out. Hit and run. Sheraton airport pickup, gym time, hot bath, room service, night sleep and off to airport again. Bam. Bam. Bam. In fact I spent more time in the embassy of Pakistan for Visa application than I actually stayed in the country. I needed to go 4 times there. And every time when I told a British-Pakistani friend I need to go again to the embassy he always said: "Karachi, Karachi – that's the price of Pakistan paradise." But country point is country point and all the efforts needed to be done.

Handicap birthday party in Frankfurt

Just some weeks after this adventure I made a front flip in a training ride and was happy to survive the 45 km/h 9 percent descent fall with a fracture of my right shoulder. No sports for three months though. All I had planned well: First Ironman Triathlon in Frankfurt, Germany at 3rd July including birthday party and then off to pacific island hopping with lean body for great face book pictures and attracting peeps. Females though! But due to accident I was the one arm bandito with a sling. Race: No! - Birthday party and travelling: Yes!

Kids cuddling in Helsinki

Since I didn't want to see other people racing in Frankfurt while I couldn't, I booked a night flight to Helsinki on my birthday. Ok, 15 hours stay for around 400 Euros is a bit expensive. But visiting friends and my own god daughters, any price should be alright. Plus I calculated free accommodation, food, drinks and fun. That would balance out all the other costs. And again Germany was playing soccer against Italy. European Championship Quarter finals. When departing it was 0:0 Germany – Italy. On arrival 2 stewardess and 5 remaining guests grouped around a little smart phone to follow the penalty shootout. All other, apparently Finish, guests had left the plane already. But the Germans were keen to suffer until the end. All the top stars like Schweinsteiger failed but the newbies in the German team made sure to have finally a success against the Italians in a big tournament. A perfect birthday present to me. Thank you very much indeed!

Australian Defense against refugees in Nauru

After this short stay in Helsinki with a champagne breakfast, hugs for my god daughters, and a situation update to my finish friends, I was off to the pacific via Frankfurt and Brisbane. Nauru should be the next destination! To Nauru people only come for collecting the country point, expats for work, or as refugees. On arrival I had 143 countries in my book. Relatively proud, I believed that I might never meet a person who has travelled as much. Of course there are other crazy peeps out there spending thousands of dollars, thousands of hours at airports or in airplanes just to get to new countries, places, territories. But these are relatively few. Some people say more people went to space than travelled to all the countries. Quick Wikipedia checkup gave the credentials of more than 600 people who flew higher than 100 kilometers above sea level which qualifies as a space trip. But only sub 50 people have made it to all 194 UN Countries. However, on arrival I met a Canadian – Chinese guy that had around 170 UN states. He also came to this place to tick off this country. We decided to spend our common travel time together on this island and to do the sightseeing together. All the way we could exchange our hero stories from around the globe. Luckily he was well prepared for Nauru. He knew the island has a surrounding of just 20 kilometers, is rich on phosphates, and there lots of refugee camps. In addition, old WW II military equipment can be found. Indeed the beaches were not for swimming. The mineral stones in the sand didn't bring up a Thai beach feeling. But great pictures were guaranteed because of the strange rock formations in combination with trees, sandy beaches, and wavy sea water. For sports people: A half marathon for breakfast is easy peasy done just by going around this tiny island.

Marshall- Dream islands of the Pacific

Off to the Marshall Islands. My reception was rain, rain, rain. Not a good start for a nice island feeling. On arrival I met another country collector. When this American fellow saw my suit case full of flag stickers at the airport he directly asked how many countries I already had. He had impressive 182 and looked like being in his mid 30ies. Only left were great places like Turkey, Greece, Iceland and war zones like Syria. I just arrived in places that I didn't really know 5 years ago and I met people only travelling to places just because they exist and to fulfill their dreams of having done it all. But on the other hand I felt like a slight beginner at running a marathon of 6 hours and talking to a pro athlete with a 2.10 finish when I meet people like this American. Not only had he more countries, but he is also well educated on how to use mileages to get rewards and is hunting all the UNESCO Heritage sites worldwide. Before coming to the pacific I was happy and proud about the achievement but in just 2 days I was grounded. However, better not comparing with others otherwise travel depression would kick in. Or at least, finding a proper balance in this regard.

No swim is no solution

The next day spending on ENEKO Island via a day tour. Luckily the sun was up, 30 degrees and the beach was a dream. Top, Crystal clear water, and great for swimming. But due to my injury I couldn't really enjoy the water since the wing was still damaged and it hurt when I moved it. Nevertheless, using the time to relax and walk around. Flex time. Later in the day I met that American guy again per chance and spontaneously we went for dinner to exchange travel stories. Maybe there is one or another travel recommendation I could get from him for cheap flights, sightseeing spots and other travel highlights. Since we got along very well there was a quick agreement on the German-American travel bond also for the next days in Kiribati.

Battle island of Kiribati

I quickly became aware that my travel companion was playing in another league of travelling. With proper GPS on his smart phone and deep knowledge of the island including all WW II memorial sights he was so much better prepared than me. I didn't do any research in advance. I only wanted the country point, maybe a bit running and walking and seeing what's coming up. I planned to book day trips and go with the pacific island flow. Travelling can be either way: Deep or rough planning, spontaneous action, or well prepared tours. However, travelling by local busses and walking through WW II battle fields with lots of tanks, and guns, at the beaches brought back the bloody history. Now kids play in-between these metallic monuments and other relicts from the Japanese/American conflicts of the last century. And if the sun is setting in the right moment the atmosphere is stunning.

Catwalk for ladies in Minsk

Bam!. New countries. Check!. Then back to Europe. Another 16 hours flight, two Gin and Tonics, and some movies before arrival in Frankfurt. A short family visit, then again into another Airbus Flyer. Off to Minsk, the Capital of Belarus. My Russian Friend Sergey recommended this place like this: "Hey man, you should look for your future wife over there". There is a majority of hot women. Like in Ukraine!" Ok. We will see. And I saw! Even from the taxi I could spot the wide streets, the massive buildings and the long legs for the thin, well dressed ladies. It seems the women use the wide sidewalks as a runway for showing off, with all that they got – whith short skirts and high heels. Men? Only a few. Women – Men ratio 70:30. And it was 3 pm in the afternoon during the week. Maybe the men are working to get some cash for affording all the women including their outfits and their bodies. Who knows? After a quick shower in my boutique hotel I crashed into a wedding in the ground floor, got a photograph with the bride and groom and headed off to downtown.

Island hopping from beach to beach

Once you reach the Pacific you might have seen already the beaches of Thailand, Dubai, Seychelles, and Maldives. Therefore, it's good to hop from island to island to get fresh impressions. There are always differences in palm trees, currents, sand, stones, underwater flora and fauna etc. Especially on this trip there was the geological island of Nauru, but if you are more in for military equipment from World War II then you need to head to Kiribati and the Marshall Islands.

Antarctica: To the end of the world

At the end of the year I finally made it to the last continent. 10 days trip into the Antarctica. Ok, it is not a country but a continent. After that I would have done it all. I believed I would see the snow, ice, penguins, different birds, and sea lions. So I thought it might be a bit boring because I am not an animal lover aside of having them served medium on a plate. As well, photo shoots are only for Facebook quality and it is also not my hobby. Nevertheless, running the marathon there would be too expensive yet for me. So I booked a trip with

Quark Expeditions leaving from Southern Argentina.

When angels travel they get an upgrade

Since I was short on budget I booked the cheapest category. I still needed money for other country points of course. So I got: 3 people in total in one indoor cabin. No window. Sharing with 2 strangers for 6000 US Dollar plus another 800 for the connection flight from Buenos Aires to Ushuaia, the harbor fees for disembarking, including one night in a 5 star hotel in BA. I had also booked in advance a night stay over outside in Antarctica and a mountaineering tour. But three weeks before the trip kicked off I got an upgrade worth 4000 US Dollars: Room share only with 1 person plus having a little window to see Antarctica from the room. Super! Oh so I could take with me another female theoretically since I was single again at that point of time. But all requests were denied and excuses came in no time; no money, no vacation, different priorities. However I strongly believe all these peeps will never make it. Paradise they will never see. If you want to reach something special in life you have to make also some special moves –

especially outside the box of comfortability. Even better, getting some fun onboard anyways.

Globetrotter meets travel rookie

At the check-in desk of the 5 Star hotel in Buenos Aires the night before the flight down to Ushuaia to the cruise boat I met my roommate, a young American boy in his early 20ies. The young investment banker had seen only three or four countries but me over 150 in total. "Why not go directly to Antarctica?" –was his response to my question why he was going in his early travel years to the 7th continent. So what will come after? Booking a flight to Mount Everest or directly to space? If he wants to increase the level of travelling then it will be really hard to top it. To get along with each other I took him out for a sightseeing bus ride, some wine and of course a steak house. Argentina without wine and steak – impossible. 800 gram steak for dinner. Bam! As a hobby vegetarian I had to sacrifice. Travel hospitality has a higher priority than some calories. I am not every weekend in Argentina as well. I also agreed on having one or two glasses of red wine, even knowing another ironman will be coming up soon. When not training correctly all the time, then at least the nutrition should be ok. At the end we had killed three bottles. The youngster finished two of them. The last was for me. But for me as his theoretical dad and sportsperson the impact of food and drinks were tremendous. All in during the evening in the restaurant, all out during the night at the rest room. I am not used to stuff like that anymore.

Upper class travels to the south

Lucky me: No hangover on next morning. Only a small coffee and a croissant for breakfast, then meet all the other adventure people in the lobby of the hotel. Strangely all people that were sitting in the bus around us were the core travel mates for the next 10 days on the boat. It was a colorful mix of people: An older grandpa like guy working as psychologist, my roommate the travel greenhorn, a blonde young New Yorker girl, a Boston tough lady in her 30ies (look alike of Michelle Obama) and Mister Shorty – a family day guy travelling alone always wearing shorts. All American! Awesome peeps.

Superb service onboard

After the short flight to the south of Argentina, I got my first surprise onboard the "The ocean Endeavour". This excursion boat was one of a higher class. The service was great. Twice a day a maid came to clean the cabin, made the beds and tidied up. Every time a little piece of chocolate was sitting on the pillow. These are the small things in travel life that make the difference. In addition, on top was the Indulgement in the restaurant. 3 course dinner every evening with the choice of different dishes for each course. Beer and wine on a refill basis included. Before the trip I planned 1 glass of wine a day but this quickly turned into a bottle a day. Social drinking rules! The better the travel company the better and harder the drinking. I directly gave a compliment to the chef of the restaurant: "I expected penguins, snow and ice but not this excellent service."

Adventure stories from the cold continent

Here in the Antarctic I had so many first timers: Stand up paddle boarding, mountaineering, and camping in the ice. I could even do Judo with a real Japanese guy – also a black belt, while the little sweet penguins were passing by. I told this story to my fellow travelers and promptly had to teach them one session onboard. But the real highlight came on day 3: The polar plunge. We stopped in a silent, calm bay. No wind. Sun was up. Blue sky. 4 degrees Celsius. My cabin mate told me there will be the jump into the ice cold water. In the beginning I wasn't that happy about it. Water is not my element. And cold water I hate. Usually I swim in 30 degrees Celsius pool water in Riyadh. But everything went really quickly. Bath robe and swim wear on and lining up with around 80 people getting ready to jump, saved from falling overboard by a rope. All these guys wanted to have this polar plunge. I thought: "When even the old retired people jump, or the young ladies, me as an Ironman have to do the same." The social pressure was on. When all people jump, I do the same.

Screaming in the ice of eternity

Finally it was my turn. I made a step forward. I screamed. I was a bit afraid somehow. Platsch. I was in the water. Instinctively I started swimming. I stayed in the water for around 20 minutes. One of the crew members asked me to do the butterfly. But for years I didn't learn it so far. Damn! But then I got a little panicked since I knew getting a shock in the cold can happen ad-hoc. So I made my way to the safety stairs. Quickly out, and into some warm dry clothes.

The best restaurant in the world

What happened next is one of the best travel moments in my life. On the rear deck the crew had arranged a BBQ a la après ski parties with Jagertee, nice electro music, hot grilled meat, and pork sausages. In combination with the stunning landscape, the cold, the icebergs, the snow and all the happy plunge survivors – breathtaking. Using the word "wonderful" for explaining travelling experience would make you ashamed if you haven't been to the Antarctic before. After this trip it is hard to use this term. Definitely this trip brings travelling to the next level.

2017 and beyond

If I didn't die from Ebola, plane crash or heart attacks I still do travelling. Upcoming plans are already made: Ticking off the last UN recognized countries until end of 2018 and visiting some breakaway countries such as Taiwan, Somaliland or South Ossetia. And after that there are inhabitant territories that I want to visit7 summits? Maybe. North Pole could be an option as well. And once the prices for space flights drop – that's the next goal for the next 5 to 10 years. But in parallel planning already bringing little projects to life.

Rumble in the jungle of Brazil

So I plan to visit the rural area of Praia de Tupeclose to Manaus in Brazil. In Saudi I met another German fellow Christian that is married to a local native Brazilian woman, having 2 kids and acting as the local medicine man. I just call him the white Shaman since Christian seems not having seen sunlight for ages. Together we plan to build a little capoeira school for the kids and maybe building a hostel of travelers around the globe. I give Brazil a second chance after I didn't really like it in the first place.

Travel opportunities in Saudi Arabia

Another option is to discover more of the inside of the Kingdom of Saudi Arabia. In Riyadh I got a French friend whose passion is to travel inside the country, with a special focus on history and archeology. For me visiting such places once or twice would be enough. Seen that, been there, done that. Check! But Florent wants to explore always further each area to discover more incredible landscapes and ancient rock art. I couldn't believe. But actually he gained lots of knowledge by it. I guess he is the best travelled person in Saudi Arabia. He often takes other expat friends with him on his trips to show the unexpected beauty of the landscape of Saudi Arabia. He has also set up a website to show to the world what Saudi Arabia is really about. It is called The Saudi Arabia Tourism Guide and it has become a reference in terms of tourism in the country. And just in 2017 the travel restrictions for Non-Muslim tourists were lifted in accordance to the modernization and opening process of Saudi Arabia. What a great opportunity for worldwide travelers!